WILLIAM A. BARRY, S.J.

GOD'S PASSIONATE AND DESIRE OUR RESPONSE

AVE MARIA PRESS Notre Dame, Indiana 46556

"The Story" by Brendan Kennelly is reprinted by permission of Bloodaxe Books Ltd., from: *A Time for Voices: Selected Poems 1960-1990* by Brendan Kennelly (Bloodaxe Books, Newcastle Upon Tyne, England, 1990).

"Scaffolding" and "Storm on an Island" are taken from *Death of a Naturalist* by Seamus Heaney. Copyright Faber & Faber Limited, London. Used with permission.

Excerpts from *An Interrupted Life* by Etty Hillesum, trans. by Arno Pomerans; English translation copyright © 1983 by Jonathan Cape, Ltd. Reprinted by permission of Pantheon Books, a division of Random House, Inc.

Scripture quotations are from the *New Revised Standard Version Bible*, copyright 1989 by the Division of Christian Education of the National Council of Churches of Christ in the USA. Used with permission.

Chapters 1, 12, and 17 first appeared in *America*. Chapters 2, 4, 7, and 10 first appeared in *The Tablet*. Chapters 6, 11, and 14 first appeared in *Human Development*. Permission to use these materials is gratefully acknowledged.

International Standard Book Number: 0-87793-501-7
0-87793-500-9 (pbk.)

Library of Congress Catalog Card Number: 92-75346

Cover and text design by Elizabeth J. French

Cover photograph by Justin A. Soleta

Printed and bound in the United States of America.

GOD'S PASSIONATE

AND
OUR

DESIRE

RESPONSE

To my dear friends
John T. Carmody and Denise Lardner Carmody
lovers of and witnesses to the mystery we call God

"And Thou like adamant draw mine iron heart."
John Donne

Acknowledgments

Many people have helped me to put together these meditations. The many who confided in me their experiences of God and of resistance to God go unnamed, but they know how integral to this book they are and how grateful I am. I want to say a special thanks to my own spiritual director, Anne Harvey, S.N.D., who with great patience and insight has helped me to see where I was resisting the pull of my own deepest desire. Once again I express my gratitude to my father and sisters for their fidelity to reading my stuff and commenting favorably on it and to Marika Geogeghan, my dear friend, who reads both critically and encouragingly. During the writing of most of this book I have been provincial of the Jesuits of the New England Province. That I have been able to write at all during this year is due to the quality of the Jesuits of my province who make it relatively easy to be provincial and especially to the staff who work with me at the Provincial Offices all of whom make it a pleasure to enter the office and make my job easier and even enjoyable. Finally I am grateful to Frank Cunningham and the editorial staff of Ave Maria Press who have worked so well to help me make my work more accessible to others.

Of course, the deepest debt of gratitude is to God who like adamant draws our iron hearts and who also gives me the ability to write at all and the privilege to write about the most important relationship any of us will ever have. *Laus Deo semper.*

Contents

Foreword

Readers familiar with my writing on prayer know that I am fascinated by the deep desire planted in each of us for union with God and, in connection with that, union with one another. At the same time I continually note in myself and in those who have confided in me a strong resistance to the fulfillment of that desire, a fulfillment, it seems, passionately desired by God. The poet and cleric John Donne has expressed the ambivalence of the human heart in the last line of the first of his *Holy Sonnets* in these words: "And Thou like adamant draw mine iron heart." This line, which will introduce the third of these meditations, has also suggested the theme of this book on our relationship with God and its consequences. God is the "adamant," the lodestone which continually attracts our "iron hearts." The fact that the poet uses the adjective "iron" indicates, I believe, the ambivalence of our hearts. On the one hand as "iron" they are attracted by the "adamant"; on the other hand, iron is not a malleable material unless it is molten. And often our hearts are cold indeed.

Some of these meditations have appeared in magazines. People have told me that they were helpful. Other meditations appear here for the first time. I hope that they will be of help to those who are drawn like iron to the adamant who is God. I suggest that we make our own the prayer of Anselm of Canterbury in the first chapter of his *Proslogion* (modified from the first person singular to the first person plural):

11

Teach us to seek you, and reveal yourself to us as we seek; for unless you instruct us we cannot seek you, and unless you reveal yourself we cannot find you. Let us seek you in desiring you; let us desire you in seeking you. Let us find you in loving you; let us love you in finding you.

Part 1

Foundations

Chapter 1

Founding Our Relationship With God

God desires a relationship with us. Can we apply what we know of human relationships to our relationship with God?

In his poem entitled "Scaffolding," Seamus Heaney uses the metaphor of scaffolding to say something profound about his relationship to a loved one. The couple in the poem have built the wall of their love so solidly that they do not need the scaffolding any more. I want to develop the metaphor so that we can see its application.

> Masons, when they start upon a building,
> Are careful to test out the scaffolding;
>
> Make sure that planks won't slip at busy points,
> Secure all ladders, tighten bolted joints.
>
> And yet all this comes down when the job's done
> Showing off walls of sure and solid stone.
>
> So if, my dear, there sometimes seem to be
> Old bridges breaking between you and me
>
> Never fear. We may let the scaffolds fall
> Confident that we have built our wall.
>
> —from *Death of a Naturalist*

15

First, let's look at the development of a strong relationship between two human beings. What might be the scaffolding necessary for it? I am reminded of the fox who asked Saint-Exupéry's Little Prince to become his friend. The Little Prince wants to know how to go about it, and the fox replies:

> You must be very patient. First you will sit down at a little distance from me—like that—in the grass. I shall look at you out of the corner of my eye, and you will say nothing . . . but you will sit a little closer to me, every day. . . .

The next day when the Prince comes, the fox tells him:

> It would have been better to come back at the same hour [so that he can anticipate his arrival]. If you come at just any time, I shall never know at what hour my heart is to be ready to greet you . . . One must observe the proper rites. [The French is more concise: *Il faut des rites.*]

Earlier in the conversation the fox says:

> One only understands the things that one tames [befriends]. Men have no more time to understand anything. They buy things all ready made at the shops. But there is no shop anywhere where one can buy friendship, and so men have no friends any more.

In these days of "instant friendship" such attention to "rites" may seem arcane and a bit romantic. Television and film seem to require little more for love between a man and a woman than a passionate look before the couple are in bed together. The fact that committed relationships of marriage or friendship seem more the exception than the norm may reveal the bankruptcy of the culture of instant relationships. Perhaps Saint-Exupéry is not so romantic after all. Perhaps "rites are necessary."

Father Joseph Flanagan, S.J. of Boston College has noted on a number of occasions that Americans have lost the "rites" of dating and courting. When those of us who are over fifty were growing up, we had a pretty good idea of how to act with the opposite sex. It was a somewhat daunting prospect to begin the process of developing a relationship, but we knew the rites, as it were. Now many young people are at sea because there are few guidelines, few accepted ways of acting that allow a gradual development of intimacy. As a result young students beginning university are barraged with courses and talks about the use of alcohol and drugs, about date rape, about racial and sexual stereotyping. But most of the input is information. What seems terribly lacking are generally accepted rites of passage and standards of moral behavior that can guide young people as they explore new relationships and learn the ways of intimacy and friendship. We need to develop ways of establishing ties, of getting close to or befriending one another. It takes time and requires "rites." These rites are the scaffolding that builds the wall of a sound and lasting friendship.

What are some of the rites? First, there has to be an attraction between two people. Only when I find you attractive, will I want to get to know you better. Then come the rites. I try to spend time with you, perhaps at first seemingly by accident. But as it becomes apparent that the attraction is mutual, we will make time to be with each other, to do things together. We will gradually reveal things about ourselves to each other. Finally, when both of us are relatively sure of the depth of our friendship, we might formalize what has become a reality. We begin to be steady dates, or we affirm that we are best friends, or in some other way acknowledge that we are special to one another. In the process of building our "wall" we may have some difficult times, times when we miscommunicate, when we quarrel, when one or the other of us feels afraid of not being appreciated. We are, after all, human beings with all the foibles and fears we are heir to. We may each be as skittish as the fox in Saint-Exupéry's story. But once we have established ties, once we have befriended

17

each other, then "we may let the scaffold fall / Confident that we have built our wall."

Now let's see what might follow in our relationship with God. The analogy limps on the side of God, but holds up quite well as far as we are concerned. We know from revelation that we exist because God desires us into being and keeps us in being. God, it would seem, is madly in love with us, is always attracted to us. The problem is that most of us do not really believe it. Many of us harbor an image of God as a taskmaster or even a tyrant because of psychological traumata or poorly assimilated teaching about God. As a result the desire for God which is implanted deep in our hearts by creation itself is often muted, if not smothered, by fear of God. We need experiences of God as attractive. We have to give God a chance to prove to us that God really is our heart's love and desire.

As C. S. Lewis noted in his autobiography, *Surprised by Joy*, every so often we are overcome by a feeling of enormous well-being and a desire for "we know not what." This desire is what he calls joy, and he describes it as more satisfying than the fulfillment of any other desire even though we recognize that this desire cannot be fully satisfied this side of heaven. We need to recall and savor these experiences of "joy" so that we will want to develop an intimate relationship of friendship and love with God. I have come to believe that these experiences are experiences of our own creation. Moreover, I believe, they are the experiences that led Ignatius of Loyola to formulate his First Principle and Foundation at the beginning of the *Spiritual Exercises*. In this rather abstract statement, Ignatius spells out the implications of experiencing that we are all created with the desire for union with God and that nothing but such union will satisfy us.

Here is an example of the welling up of such a desire in an ordinary experience, one that any teen-ager might have. In his autobiography, *Sacred Journey*, Frederick Buechner tells of an experience he had in Bermuda where his mother had taken him and his brother after his father's tragic suicide. At thirteen, near the end of his stay, he was sitting with a girl of thirteen on a wall watching ferries come and go. Quite innocently, he says,

> Our bare knees happened to touch for a moment, and in that moment I was filled with such a sweet panic and anguish of longing for I had no idea what that I knew my life could never be complete until I found it. . . . It was the upward-reaching and fathomlessly hungering, heart-breaking love for the beauty of the world at its most beautiful, and, beyond that, for that beauty east of the sun and west of the moon which is past the reach of all but our most desperate desiring and is finally the beauty of Beauty itself, of Being itself and what lies at the heart of Being.

Buechner himself notes that there are many ways of looking at this experience. He recognizes the possibilities of psychological and sexual influences. He goes on to say that "looking back at those distant years I choose not to deny, either, the compelling sense of an unseen giver and a series of hidden gifts as not only another part of their reality, but the deepest part of all."

Many people have such experiences, researchers tell us, but not many people savor them and reflect on them and draw the implications of them for their lives. Ignatius did all these things. What he came to see is that these experiences show that God creates each human being for union with the triune God and that nothing but union with that creative purpose of God will satisfy us in this life or in the next. From such experiences and from his theological studies Ignatius came to see that the universe is a place where God is continually drawing each and every one of us into the community life of the Trinity. It is as though the three Persons in God, the perfect community of Father, Son, and Holy Spirit, say to one another: "Our community life is so rich and satisfying. Why don't we create a universe where we can invite other persons into our community life?"

Ignatius invites us to take seriously these foundational experiences of God creating us out of love and for a loving community. For such a pearl we would want nothing to get in the way, which is what Ignatius meant by the notion of being indifferent to all created things. Not that we do not care for things, but rather that we do not want to be so attached to any of them that we would miss the pearl of great price, which is to be in tune with God's creative purpose in creating the universe and each one of us.

Once our desire for a more intimate relationship with God is aroused, then we need to take time to let God draw us closer. Like the fox we may feel a bit skittish with God. If so, we could tell God to take it slowly so as not frighten us off. Such a statement is a wonderfully honest prayer. Even if we are somewhat fearful, we are attracted to a deeper relationship with God. We can also tell God that fact. Still, we do need to make time for God to draw us closer. Again we might take a leaf from the advice of the fox and set aside a particular time each day or each week for the encounter with God. The time does not have to be long, but it is good to be regular. *Il faut des rites.* I would also suggest that we be clear about our desires, and about the ambivalence of our desires. Even though every human being is constantly being drawn by divine love toward union with God, still we all have conflicting desires as well. Fear gets in the way of our desire to become more intimate with God. Hurts from our past may leave us unsure whether we can really trust God with our future. At this stage, as at any stage, of our journey toward God honesty is the best policy. Telling God about our deep ambivalence, and then listening for God's response, is part of the process of building the wall of our friendship.

In these early stages of a developing intimacy with God the "rites" of time and place and manner of prayer are the scaffolding necessary for establishing the solidity of the friendship. Prayer books and books on prayer can also be helpful as scaffolding. In religious congregations novitiates are places where structures and time orders are more needed. These are the scaffolding necessary for building the wall that is a way of life. When the wall is built, then the scaffolding can gradually be let fall. So too in a developing relationship with God, when the ties are relatively firmly established, the rites necessary at the beginning can be dropped. Indeed, a slavish holding on to the rites may be an indication that the relationship has not been well established. In our developing relationship with God there comes a time when "we may let the scaffolds fall / Confident that we have built our wall."

Chapter 2

Why Do We Pray?

We have always heard that we need to pray to foster our relationship with God, but why?

Recently I attended a workshop on the "relaxation response" led by Herbert Benson, M.D. and his associates. Dr. Benson has found that this "response" is physiologically the opposite of the "fight or flight response." In times of perceived danger the output of adrenaline causes an increase of the body's metabolism, higher blood pressure, rate of breathing and heart rate and faster brain waves. These physiological changes prepare the organism to fight or to flee the danger. The opposite reactions, lower blood pressure, rate of breathing and heart rate and slower brain waves, Benson calls the "relaxation response." Since prolonged exposure to stress can lead to many kinds of physical and psychological illnesses, the relaxation response has beneficial physical and psychological effects. He has found that this response is induced by meditation, the kind of meditation taught by the late John Main, O.S.B., and his followers and called "centering prayer" by the Trappist Basil Pennington. Benson has shown that such meditation has beneficial effects on a person's physical and psychological health.

This workshop once again brought up for me the question: Why do we pray? Do we pray for utilitarian reasons? For example, do we pray because it benefits our physical or psychological health?

Honesty compels me to say that I often do pray for utilitarian reasons. First of all, most petitionary prayers ask for some good result either for myself or for someone else or for all people. Moreover, I feel contented that I have remembered people who mean much to me even if my prayer is not answered. I notice, too, that I feel better about myself when I pray regularly. I feel more centered, more in tune with the present, less anxious about the past or the future. So I suspect that I do pray for utilitarian reasons. But does that exhaust my motivations for prayer? Once again, thinking of prayer as conscious relationship may be illuminating.

Why do we spend time with good friends? As I pondered this question, I realized that I relish times with good friends for some of the same reasons just adduced for spending time in prayer. If I have not had good conversations with close friends for some time, I feel out of sorts, somewhat lonely, and ill at ease. When I am with good friends, I feel more whole and alive. Still I do not believe that my only reason for wanting time with them is to feel better. I am genuinely interested in and concerned for them. I want to be with them because I love them. The fact that being with them has beneficial effects on me is a happy by-product. I do not believe that it is my principal motive. Moreover, I have often spent time with friends when it cost me trouble and time, and I did it because they wanted my presence. Haven't we all spent time with a close friend who was ill or depressed even when the time was painful and difficult? Sometimes we do not recognize or believe in our own real love of the other for the other's sake.

Of course, there are times when we need the presence of close friends because we are in pain or lonely. Friendship would not be a mutual affair if we were always the ones who gave and never were open to receive. But if we are not totally egocentric, we will have to admit that we do care for others for their own sakes, and not just for what we can get from the relationship. Can we say the same thing about our relationship with God?

Before we look at the positive side of the analogy, let's notice where it limps, and badly. All human relationships, no matter how one-sided they may seem, are based on mutual need. To be anywhere near our best selves we need people who love us. As infants every one of us needs others to love and care for us. Without some caretaker we would die, and without a caretaker who shows care, we would not develop as persons. Our dependence on others to be ourselves continues throughout life even if that dependence becomes lessened as we grow up. But even the parents upon whom the infant relies totally need the infant in some way, even if only as the consummation of their love for each other. God, however, does not need anyone else. God, Father, Son and Spirit, is the perfect community. They need nothing else for their completion. We must not succumb to the romantic notion that God decided to create a universe with other persons in it because God was lonely. Rather, as we have said, it is as though the three Persons say to one another, "Our community life is so good, why don't we create other persons and invite them into this life?" God does not create out of need, but out of love.

Even though God does not create out of need, this does not mean that a relationship of mutuality is impossible. Such relationships are created by intention and desire, not by need. Even our human relationships of mutual love and friendship rest on intention and desire much more than on need. Of course, I need my friends, but if neediness is the prevailing motivation, then fear for myself if I lose them predominates over love for them. If God invites us into the community life of the Trinity, then God desires a relationship of mutuality with us.

The Hebrew Bible gives some indications of such an intention on God's part. In Genesis we get the impression that before the fall God walked and conversed with Adam and

Eve in the cool of the evening. Also we can look at the Abraham cycle of stories in Genesis 12-18 as a saga of a growing mutual relationship between Abraham and God, culminating in God's decision to tell Abraham what God intends to do to Sodom and Gomorrah: "Shall I hide from Abraham what I am about to do?" (Gn 18:17). God's revelation of his intention to destroy the cities leads to Abraham's haggling with God to save them. Abraham goes so far in mutuality as to tell God how God should act. "Far be it from you to do such a thing, to slay the righteous with the wicked, so that the righteous fare as the wicked! Far be that from you! Shall not the Judge of all the earth do what is just?" (v. 25).

In the gospel of John Jesus tells his disciples (and through them us): "I do not call you servants any longer, because the servant does not know what the master is doing; but I have called you friends, because I have made known to you everything that I have heard from my Father" (Jn 15:15). He then goes on to underline the notion of his intention when he says: "You did not choose me but I chose you. And I appointed you to go and bear fruit, fruit that will last" (v. 16). Throughout the history of Christianity men and women have discovered to their wonder and delight that God wants an intimate mutual relationship with them.

Now relationships of mutuality (friendships) are characterized by mutual transparency. Jesus makes this clear in the passage from John's gospel. He wants to be transparent to his friends. And what he reveals is his very intimate life, his life of union with the Father and the Spirit. To Philip's request that he show them the Father, Jesus replies: "Have I been with you all this time Philip, and you still do not know me? Whoever has seen me has seen the Father" (Jn 14:9). Throughout the last discourse in John's gospel Jesus reveals in a variety of ways his own inner life culminating in the final prayer in chapter 17. Christians believe that Jesus is still revealing who he is and thus who God is to all those who are willing to pay attention. Ignatius of Loyola, for example, took it so for granted that Jesus wants to reveal himself to us that he suggests to retreatants in the "Second Week" of the *Spiritual Exercises* that they ask for what they desire, namely "an intimate knowledge of our Lord, who has become human for me, that I may love Him more and follow Him more closely" (n. 104).

It works the other way as well. People who take seriously the invitation to an intimate relationship with God find that God wants them to reveal themselves as well. God wants to know our hopes and dreams, our loves and hates, our fears and anxieties. What astounds us is that God seems to be pleased when we are transparent, even when what we reveal about ourselves seems unsavory or unsuitable to say. God does not stand on protocol with us. The community that is the Trinity seems to be delighted with our willingness to trust in their desire for mutuality. Even when a person tells God how angry he or she is with God, God listens with interest and sympathy. God desires to know us just as much as we desire to know God.

Now we return to the question of why we pray. Deep within each one us sits a desire for union with Mystery itself. As we saw, C. S. Lewis called this desire joy and described it as a desire that was more satisfying and delightful than any fulfillment short of heaven itself. That desire, we can say, is the Holy Spirit of God dwelling in our hearts who draws us to the perfect fulfillment for which we were created, namely community with the Trinity. That desire draws us toward a more and more intimate union with God. Created out of love, we are drawn by the desire for "we know not what," for the ultimate Mystery who alone will satisfy our deepest longing. We pray, then, at our deepest level because we are drawn by the bonds of love. We pray because we love, and not for any utilitarian reason. If prayer has beneficial effects—and I believe that it does—that is because prayer corresponds to our deepest reality. When we are in tune with God, we cannot help but experience deep well-being. Ignatius of Loyola spoke of consolation as a sign of a person's being in tune with God's intention. But in the final analysis, the lover does not spend time with the beloved because of the consolation; the lover just wants to be with the beloved.

Another motive for prayer is the desire to praise and thank our beloved God because of God's great kindness and mercy. In contemplating Jesus we discover that God's love not only is creative but also is overwhelmingly self-sacrificing. Jesus loved us even as we human beings nailed him to the cross.

If we allow the desire for "we know not what" to draw us more and more into a relationship of mutual love with God, then we will, I believe, gradually appropriate as our own that wonderful prayer so dear to St. Francis Xavier, which begins *O Deus, ego amo te; nec amo te ut ames me*: "O God, I love you; and I do not love you so that you might love me." Gerard Manley Hopkins translated the prayer:

> O God, I love thee, I love thee—
> Not out of hope of heaven for me
> Nor fearing not to love and be
>   In the everlasting burning.
> Thou, thou, my Jesus, after me
>   Didst reach thine arms out dying,
> For my sake sufferedst nails and lance,
> Mocked and marrèd countenance,
>   Sorrows passing number,
>   Sweat and care and cumber,
> Yea and death, and this for me,
>   And thou couldst see me sinning:
> Then I, why should not I love thee,
> Jesu so much in love with me?
> Not for heaven's sake; not to be
> Out of hell by loving thee;
> Not for any gains I see;
> But just the way that thou didst me
> I do love and I will love thee:
> What must I love thee, Lord, for then?—
> For being my king and God. Amen.

Chapter 3

Attraction and Resistance

Thou hast made me, and shall Thy work decay?
Repair me now, for now mine end doth haste;
I run to death, and death meets me as fast,
And all my pleasures are like yesterday.
I dare not move my dim eyes any way,
Despair behind, and death before doth cast
Such terror, and my feeble flesh doth waste
By sin in it, which it towards hell doth weigh.
Only Thou art above, and when towards Thee
By Thy leave I can look, I rise again;
But our old subtle foe so tempteth me
That not one hour myself I can sustain.
Thy grace may wing me to prevent his art,
And Thou like adamant draw mine iron heart.

John Donne, *Holy Sonnets, 1*

In the first two meditations we have indicated that our deepest desire is for union with God, the perfect community of Father, Word, and Holy Spirit, and thus union with all other persons in that perfect community. We have noted that at times we feel the strength of that desire, the "joy" of which C. S Lewis speaks. We referred to Buechner's description of that desire as

the upward-reaching and fathomlessly hungering, heart-breaking love for the beauty of the world at its

29

most beautiful, and, beyond that, for that beauty east of the sun and west of the moon which is past the reach of all but our most desperate desiring and is finally the beauty of Beauty itself, of Being itself and what lies at the heart of Being.

Because God desires us into being in order that we may enjoy communion with God and with all persons, we desire this communion at the deepest level of our beings.

The poet and cleric John Donne knew of this desire. A number of his *Holy Sonnets* express that desire as does the very first one which we have cited at the head of this meditation. If he had not experienced the strong desire for God, he would not have made such a vehement plea as we hear in the last line of the poem: "And Thou like adamant draw mine iron heart." "Adamant," as noted in our foreword, here refers to the lodestone which acts as a magnet to iron. But the very fact that he refers to his heart as "iron" reveals what the rest of the poem almost heartbreakingly expresses: namely, that there is something in him that prevents him from moving toward the desire of his heart. He refers to his feeble flesh, to his terror of death, to sin, and to the subtle foe as forces that keep him from his heart's desire. Hence he has an "iron heart." But even though he is resistant to the attraction to God, still his "iron heart" can be magnetized by God's "adamant." Even in the midst of the deepest resistance our hearts still are strongly attracted to God, so much so that the poet can beg God to allure his heart.

The poet speaks for all of us who have tried to follow through on the deepest desire of our hearts. We all recognize that something gets in the way of attaining our desire. The resistance is easy enough to understand when we do not have a positive image of God, e.g., if God is experienced, not as desirable, but as an ogre or a judge. I have already indicated that people who have such an image of God need experiences of God as benevolent and loving, as the God who has desired each one of us into being as the apple of God's eye. However, even those of us who have had such positive experiences of God still are disconcerted, as was Donne, by our reluctance to follow up on these experiences. Even after a period of intense closeness to God, for example, we find ourselves unaccountably reluctant to engage in prayer the next day.

In a series of chapters in *Paying Attention to God* I have tried to probe the sources of such resistance. Among other sources can be numbered our fear of the consequences of getting close to God ("What will God ask me to do?"), our fear of losing control of our lives to God (as though control were in our power), our fear of losing ourselves in the immensity of God, our fear of death. Whatever the source, the resistance is real enough for anyone who takes the relationship with God seriously enough to pursue it actively.

St. Paul seems to have experienced the frustration of the resistance. In the Letter to the Romans he says: "I do not understand my own actions. For I do not do what I want, but I do the very thing I hate" (Rom 7:15) and goes on to say:

> So I find it to be a law that when I want to do what is good, evil lies close at hand. For I delight in the law of God in my inmost self, but I see in my members another law at war with the law of my mind, making me captive to the law of sin that dwells in my members. Wretched man that I am! Who will rescue me from this body of death? (v. 21-24)

I am sure that all of us can resonate with this passage. We feel the deep desire for God that responds to the magnet pull of God's desire for us, and yet we seem to do everything possible to demagnetize our hearts. We let our hearts become inordinately attached to things that do not and cannot fulfill the deepest desire of our hearts. Money, reputation, family, substances, other people become more important than the "pearl of great price." In *Addiction and Grace* Gerald May indicates that all these inordinate attachments are addictions which keep us from what we most deeply want. But precisely

because they are addictions, we feel powerless to do anything about them. Hence, Paul's cry of seeming despair,
"Wretched man that I am! Who will rescue me from this body
of death?"

But Paul answers his own question, or perhaps better the
question is answered for him. "Thanks be to God through
Jesus Christ our Lord!" (v. 25). We are not powerless. Once
we recognize that we are powerless against our addictions,
our resistances to the alluring beauty of God, then we can
turn to a "higher power," as the program of Alcoholics
Anonymous puts it. The very God who has made us for
union with the Trinity and with all persons makes it possible
for us to attain that union in spite of our resistances. Donne
puts it thus: "Only Thou art above, and when towards Thee
/ By Thy leave I can look, I rise again." God gives him the
grace to look toward God, and then, as it were, the magnetic
pull of God pulls him up from his despair.

But one time through the struggle is not the end of it. We
will, it seems, carry our resistances to union with God with
us to the grave. We wish that it could be over and done with
at one fell swoop. But usually it is not to be. Again Paul gives
us an example. In the midst of his "boasting" in the Second
Letter to the Corinthians he notes that "a thorn was given me
in the flesh, a messenger of Satan to torment me, to keep me
from being too elated" (2 Cor 12:7). We do not know what the
thorn in the flesh was, but we can interpret it for our purposes
as the continuance of the resistance to the pull of God toward
union. Paul goes on: "Three times I appealed to the Lord
about this, that it would leave me, but he said to me, 'My
grace is sufficient for you, for power is made perfect in
weakness'" (v. 8-9). In other words, we must continually rely
on our "higher power," on the "adamant" who has made us
for union and will not let us rest until we reach it.

In another powerful sonnet John Donne describes the
human dilemma in a series of paradoxes. It is a wonderful

prayer for all of us who experience the pain of desiring God but at the same time of resisting the drawing power of God.

> Batter my heart, three-personed God; for You
> As yet but knock, breathe, shine, and seek to mend;
> That I may rise and stand, o'erthrow me, and bend
> Your force to break, blow, burn, and make me new.
> I, like an usurped town, to another due,
> Labor to admit You, but O, to no end;
> Reason, Your viceroy in me, me should defend,
> But is captived, and proves weak or untrue.
> Yet dearly I love You, and would be lovèd fain,
> But am betrothed unto Your enemy.
> Divorce me, untie or break that knot again;
> Take me to You, imprison me, for I,
> Except you enthrall me, never shall be free,
> Nor ever chaste, except You ravish me.
>
> *Holy Sonnets, 14*

.

Chapter 4

Can We Really Trust God?

Though the fig tree does not blossom,
and no fruit is on the vines;
though the produce of the olive fails
and the fields yield no food;
though the flock is cut off from the fold
and there is no herd in the stalls,
yet I will rejoice in the Lord;
I will exult in the God of my salvation(Hab 3:17-18).

These brave words are regularly prayed by those who use the breviary for morning prayer. The prophet Habakkuk, in the midst of a devastating war against Israel, proclaims his faith in God. Some modern parallels might be a Jew professing such trust while awaiting transport to Auschwitz, or a Cambodian during the nightmare of the "killing fields," or an Ethiopian during the latest drought and war. Those of us who pray this prayer in the comfort of our warmed rooms may miss the enormity of what we are saying. We may not even stop to ask ourselves whether such a prayer is mere whistling in the dark, an attempt by those in very bleak circumstances to reassure themselves that all will be well in spite of appearances. Are such reassuring prayers "opium for the people," as Marx would claim? In this meditation I want to look at the experiences that may lie behind this and similar prayers.

When we see the misery of those who face wasting, incurable disease, the devastation of war, the horrors of starvation, we do not, spontaneously, think of "rejoicing in the Lord," do we? Looked at from the outside, such suffering and degradation seem absolutely foreign to the notion of joy or gratitude. Indeed, to suggest to someone suffering so horribly that he or she should thank God seems at best gratuitous, at worst insensitive and condescending. No sensible person tells a mother who has just lost her only child to leukemia to thank God, to rejoice in the Lord. Indeed, so-called pastoral responses such as "God knows best" or "God has taken your baby to the realm of happiness" ring hollow and make us cringe. In the face of horror, silence and sympathy and a willingness just to be present to the horror seem the best pastoral response. Theory has little to say at these junctures and often is an affront to the reality people are facing.

The real question I would ask is whether Habakkuk was talking from theory or from experience. Since we cannot query him, perhaps we need to look to our own experiences or to the experiences of those who have suffered horribly. Do we experience joy in the midst of terrible sorrow and suffering? In effect, do we experience resurrection now? In his book *True Resurrection* H. A. Williams makes the point: "When therefore resurrection is considered in terms of past and future, it is robbed of its impact on the present." He argues strongly that the doctrine of the resurrection, if it were to have a real impact on our lives, had to be based on present experience. He goes so far as to posit: "I have long felt that theological inquiry is basically related to self-awareness and that therefore it involves a process of self-discovery." In other words, theory about God has to be based on experience. Do we have experiences of resurrection right in the midst of our suffering and dying? Do we know people who have been able to pray the prayer of Habakkuk right in the middle of their pain and loss?

Let's take the case of the Dutch Jewess, Etty Hillesum, who died in Auschwitz in 1943. Her diaries, written during the last two years of her life in the hell of Nazi-occupied Amsterdam, record an ever-deepening realization of the reality she and every Jew faced and, at the same time, an ever-deepening relationship with God which seemed to give her deep joy. A few excerpts from *An Interrupted Life* will give a flavor.

> It is sometimes hard to take in and comprehend, oh God, what those created in Your likeness do to each other in these disjointed days. But I no longer shut myself away in my room, God, I try to look things straight in the face, even the worst crimes, and to discover the small, naked human being amidst the monstrous wreckage caused by man's senseless deeds. I don't sit here in my peaceful flower-filled room, praising You through Your poets and thinkers. That would be too simple, and in any case I am not as unworldly as my friends so kindly think. Every human being has his own reality, I know that, but I am no fanciful visionary, God, no schoolgirl with a "beautiful soul." I try to face up to Your world, God, not to escape from reality into beautiful dreams— though I believe that beautiful dreams can exist beside the most horrible reality—and I continue to praise Your creation, God, despite everything.

As the certainty of the intention of the Nazis to exterminate all Jews grows in her, the willingness to confront reality also grows. In early July she writes:

> Something has crystallized. I have looked our destruction, our miserable end which has already begun in so many small ways in our daily life, straight in the eye and accepted it into my life, and my love of life has not been diminished. I am not bitter or rebellious, or in any way discouraged.... I have come to terms with life. . . . By "coming to terms with life"

I mean: the reality of death has become a definite part of my life; my life has, so to speak, been extended by death, by my looking death in the eye and accepting it, by accepting destruction as part of life and no longer wasting my energies on fear of death or the refusal to acknowledge its inevitability. It sounds paradoxical: by excluding death from our life we cannot live a full life, and by admitting death into our life we enlarge and enrich it.

Here we see someone who faces the horrors of the reality surrounding her and yet can rejoice in the Lord. We have one example of someone who could pray and mean the prayer of Habakkuk.

In a later meditation we will refer to a recollection by Father Pedro Arrupe, the late, beloved General of the Society of Jesus, of celebrating Mass in one of the poorest slums of a city in Latin America. "These people," he said, "seemed to possess nothing and yet they were ready to give of themselves to communicate joy and happiness." Another example, perhaps.

Here is an example from a poor black sharecropper from the American South who was put in jail for union activity in the 1930s. He is now an old man telling his story to Theodore Rosengarten. Being poor and black he had no expectation of receiving justice. But in jail this is what happened to him.

And all of a sudden, God stepped in my soul. Talk about hollerin and rejoicin, I just caught fire. My mind cleared up. I got so happy—I didn't realize where I was at. I lost sight on this world to a great extent. And the Master commenced a talkin to me just like a natural man. I heard these words plain . . . "Follow me and trust me for my holy righteous word." I just gone wild then, feelin a change. . . . Good God almighty, I just felt like I could have flown out the top of that jail. I commenced a shoutin bout the Lord, how good and kind and merciful He was. Freed my soul from sin. . . . Well, they had my

trial and put me in prison. The Lord blessed my soul
and set me in a position to endure it (*All God's
Dangers: The Life of Nate Shaw*).

Obviously, Nate Shaw could have prayed the words of
Habakkuk with feeling.

I have been privileged to be spiritual director to many
people. Two of them come to mind as I reflect with you about
this topic of death and resurrection and our ability to trust in
God in the midst of the horrors life often puts in our way.
Both have given me permission to use their stories in this
meditation. One woman had come to a deep sympathy for
the sufferings of Jesus on the cross. Contemplation of Jesus
on the cross brought her very strong feelings of pain and an
acute sense of the suffering of the poor and sick people to
whom she ministered. Yet she wanted nothing more than to
be close to Jesus in spite of the pain such closeness to him
caused in her.

During this period of intense contemplation of Jesus on
the cross she became aware, for the first time, of how she had
been seriously abused in her childhood. These memories
flooded her consciousness and brought back feelings of pain
and outrage and horror that she could hardly bear. Yet
through it all she felt a deep sense of being held in the loving
embrace of a mothering God, an experience that brought her
great consolation. If she tried to evade the memories or
repress them, then this consoling presence of God also left
her. It became clear to both of us that she could not experience
true resurrection without experiencing what she was being
resurrected from. She could, without pretense, pray the
prayer of Habakkuk. Indeed, she could come to the point of
accepting all that had happened to her as what had made her
who she now was, a resurrected daughter of a loving God.

Another woman had rediscovered God in the midst of
terrible suffering brought on by treatment for Hodgkin's
disease. As she described her experience, it seemed to be one

of deep joy and freedom in the depths of pain and suffering and of loss of control over her own life. She told me that she would not wish not to have had the disease. Recently she wrote to me that this experience of God had returned and described it this way.

> I have had it (the experience of God) back again this fall. It finally came to me, with blinding simplicity, that I should let my friends help me. And in accepting openheartedly what was offered unreservedly, I was rewarded with received grace, that sense of being filled up with light, of seeing truly, of being fully conscious, of being free: completely engaged with the world, yet not bound to it. Surprised by joy. How slowly, how tentatively we learn, over and over, to surrender to God's love! Perhaps this is why we humans (need to) live such long lives.

Do we not hear in these lines echoes of "Though the fig tree does not blossom . . . yet I will rejoice in the Lord"?

These examples show that it is possible to find deep consolation at the heart of deep suffering. It is possible to trust in God, to rejoice in the Lord in spite of, or indeed, because of, all the sufferings human life is heir to. But they also show that such "received grace" is not "cheap grace." The person who can say with the psalmist, "Even though I walk through the valley of the shadow of death, I fear no evil, for you are with me; your rod and your staff, they comfort me" (Ps 23:4), knows that the valley really is of the shadow of death, knows that this comfort is given precisely there and nowhere else at this particular time of his or her life. Mary Ward, a seventeenth-century nun, once said: "The pain is great, but very endurable, because He who lays on the burden also carries it."

When we contemplate Jesus on the cross, we come to the depth of the mystery of God's love for us, the depth of the mystery of God's reckless gamble to draw us into the community life which is Father, Word, and Holy Spirit. For me two of the last words of Jesus capture the mystery of the one event which is death-resurrection. "Eli, Eli, lema sabach-thani? My God, my God, why have you forsaken me?" (Mt 27:46). This expresses the depth of the pain of the crucifixion. "Father, into your hands I commend my spirit" (Lk 23:46). This expresses Jesus' ultimate trust that all is well. In the appearance to the two disciples on the road to Emmaus Jesus expresses what all the people whose experiences I have adduced would agree to: "Was it not necessary that the Messiah should suffer these things and then enter his glory?" (Lk 24:26). Jesus would not be the Messiah he now is if his life had taken a different turn. Perhaps we cannot experience the fullness of resurrection as long as we harbor resentments about what life has dealt us. Perhaps we cannot experience resurrection until, as the woman I just quoted did, we ask for the help we need and surrender wholeheartedly to God. Can we trust God? Each of us has to answer that question for ourselves, but we can help one another to give it a try by telling of our experiences when we have tried it.

Chapter 5

How Happy Are We?

Happy are we, O Israel,
for we know what is pleasing to God (Bar 4:4).

In the Old Testament we often read that the people of God are blessed because they know the law of the Lord. This fragment from the book of Baruch is only one of many instances. Another comes from the book of Nehemiah. After their return from exile the Israelites begged Nehemiah to read from the book of Moses. He read to them for the whole morning. "And all the people went their way to eat and drink and to send portions and to make great rejoicing, because they had understood the words that were declared to them" (Neh 8:12). The psalmist waxes eloquent on the wonders of knowing and obeying the law: "I delight in the way of your decrees as much as in all riches. I will meditate on your precepts, and fix my eyes on your ways. I will delight in your statutes; I will not forget your word" (Ps 119:14-16). Some time ago when I read the passage from Baruch in the liturgy of the hours, it occurred to me to ask whether it is really true that the Israelites are blessed to know what pleases God, that we Christians are blessed because of such knowledge. Are you really happier for knowing the law of the Lord?

I remembered a story told to me by an old friend from my scholastic days in Germany. Adolph is now a Jesuit priest working in Indonesia. On his way to the States he stopped in Thailand where there has been religious tolerance for hundreds of years. He asked a missionary with many years of experience in Thailand why there were so few Christians in spite of the relative freedom to preach the gospel. The missionary replied that the Thai people are a happy and contented people; if they were to become Christian, they would have to obey all the laws of the church. Adolph hit his head with his hand and exclaimed, "So much for the good news." I wonder how many of us have at times thought that we would have an easier time of it if we were not Christians or Roman Catholic Christians. Is knowledge of what pleases God really good news?

To be truthful we would have to admit that a stranger visiting most of our liturgies would wonder about our use of language when he or she heard us call them "celebrations." We do not look as though we are enjoying ourselves or celebrating anything. I wonder how many of us go regularly to Sunday liturgy because we feel that we "have to," in other words, because we know what pleases God. If we did not "have to" go, would we? We found out in a hurry how blessed Catholics felt about "going to confession." Once we found out that we did not have to do so the number of those going to the sacrament of penance or reconciliation declined dramatically. In my work as a spiritual director I have met many people whose prayer brought them no sense of being blessed, but who, when asked why they continued to try to pray, answered, "Because I have to, because God wants me to."

Apparently knowing "what pleases God" does not make everyone feel happy. Some people who live very "religious" lives do not exude a sense of happiness. A nursing nun, it was reported to me, once told a woman in labor that her pains were just recompense for the pleasure of sex. It does not sound as though the nun's renunciation of marriage and family had made her feel happy. Scrupulous people suffer a great deal trying to fulfill the least letter of the law; there is no joy in their hearts that they "know what pleases God." A friend of mine once told me that he had come to the point of hating God for making him stay in religious life; he thought that being a religious was what would please God. I was relieved when someone I was directing told me (finally) that he hated to pray and hated the God who seemed to demand that he pray. I felt that we had at last touched reality and that now he could move forward in his relationship with God.

Our reflections thus far indicate that knowledge of what pleases God may not bring on a feeling of blessedness. Some people who "know" what pleases God obviously do not exude a sense of blessedness or happiness. The knowledge that Baruch speaks of must mean more than a grudging acceptance of the "will of God" if it is to lead to blessedness. A merely external observance of God's will does not guarantee happiness. Those who obey the "will of God" grudgingly usually are not happy and very often seem to be "holier than thou" types, people who look down on those who do not live up to their own high standards. If scripture is to be believed, knowledge of what is pleasing to God and an attempt to live according to that knowledge should lead to humility, gentleness, and gratitude. Does it do so?

This question cannot be answered in the abstract or by theory. It can only be answered by each one of us from our experience. Before I give some examples of a positive answer to these questions, let me pose another question: Does it make sense to expect to feel blessed in this life at all? Again, on the face of it one is tempted to answer that it does not make sense. The central Christian symbol is the cross; Jesus suffered this horrible and demeaning death because he knew what pleases God and acted accordingly. Certainly, afterwards he was blessed in the resurrection, but during the crucifixion could anyone honestly say that he was blessed? This life is a vale of tears, is it not? And those who know what pleases God and act according to that knowledge often suffer just as Jesus suffered. There was an unspoken rule for discernment prevalent in the church in the days prior to Vatican II which indicated that the more unpalatable of two choices was the one to lean toward since it was more likely in accord with God's will. The idea that we should expect to feel happy in this life seems farfetched, does it not?

And yet, in the rules for discernment of spirits proposed by Ignatius of Loyola in the *Spiritual Exercises* we read that for

> those who go on earnestly striving to cleanse their souls from sin and who seek to rise in the service of God . . . it is characteristic of the good spirit . . . to give courage and strength, consolations, tears, inspirations, and peace. This He does by making all easy, by removing all obstacles so that the soul goes forward in doing good (n. 315).

Ignatius expects that those who know what pleases God and try to act according to this knowledge will be blessed. And Ignatius is talking from experience, his own and others', not from theory.

According to him, if we are trying to live a life in accordance with God's good pleasure, the best criterion for deciding whether an experience or a choice or a way of acting is of God or not is to ask whether we find ourselves "blessed," in the sense of having "courage and strength, consolations, tears, inspirations, and peace." This rule only echoes Paul's words to the Galatians based on his own experiences: "By contrast, the fruit of the Spirit is love, joy, peace, patience, kindness, generosity, faithfulness, gentleness and self-control" (Gal 5:22-23). In fact, in the same rule Ignatius notes that "it is characteristic of the evil spirit to harass with anxiety, to afflict with sadness, to raise obstacles backed by fallacious reasonings that disturb the soul." From his experience Ignatius, it seems, would echo the words of Baruch with which we began this meditation.

In the Sermon on the Mount Jesus himself proclaimed as blessed the poor in spirit, the brokenhearted, the meek, those who hunger and thirst for righteousness, the merciful, the pure in heart, and even the persecuted (Mt 5:3-11). Jesus was proclaiming not a theory, but a fact, a fact borne out by his experience. On the cross he did suffer terribly; the cry of anguish, "My God, my God, why have you forsaken me?" (Mt 27:46) has chilled many Christians to the marrow as they contemplated this scene in prayer. Yet, whatever the meaning of this cry, according to the gospel of Luke Jesus was still able to say, "Father, forgive them; for they do not know what they are doing" (Lk 23:34) and with his final breath, "Father, into your hands I commend my spirit" (v. 46). Such words could not come from a person who was not somehow blessed and thus able to think of others and to trust his Father. It would appear that Jesus himself experienced happiness in knowing what pleases God.

In the Acts of the Apostles we read that Peter and the other apostles were flogged by the Sanhedrin and told not to speak in the name of Jesus. "As they left the council, they rejoiced that they were considered worthy to suffer dishonor for sake of the name. And every day in the temple and at home, they did not cease to teach and proclaim Jesus as the Messiah" (Acts 5:41-42). Often in his letters Paul attests to his joy in being able to suffer for the sake of the gospel. For example: "So, I will boast all the more gladly of my weaknesses, so that the power of Christ may dwell in me. Therefore, I am content with weaknesses, insults, hardships, persecutions, and calamities for the sake of Christ; for whenever I am weak, then I am strong" (2 Cor 12:9-10). Apparently in the early church knowing what pleases God and acting according to that knowledge did bring a sense of blessedness.

Down the centuries people have found blessedness from knowing what pleases God and acting according to this knowledge, even when their actions led to their suffering and martyrdom. St. Lawrence the deacon who was burned to death is reputed to have kept his sense of humor even in his last agony. St. Ignatius of Antioch could not wait to be torn to pieces by the lions and hoped that nothing would prevent him from his martyrdom. St. Francis of Assisi rejoiced in being considered a fool for Christ. St. Ignatius of Loyola felt deep consolation when he was imprisoned by the Inquisitors. In these cases and in others the blessedness seems to have come from a deep love of and a deep identification with Jesus. Because of their great love of Jesus and their desire to follow Jesus in knowing and doing what pleases God they discovered their deepest happiness. They were indeed blessed.

In more recent times we have instances of ordinary people who have known and done what pleases God and found blessedness, even in very hard circumstances. Etty Hillesum, the young Dutch Jewess mentioned in the last meditation, recorded a deepening relationship with God in the midst of the hell that was Amsterdam occupied by the Nazis. Her diaries testify to the grace of blessedness given in the worst of circumstances. The more she came to know and live out what pleases God, the more peaceful and happy she became. Two months before her death she tells her friend Tide what she has just written in her diary: "You have made me so rich, oh God, please let me share out your beauty with open hands."

Bishop Oscar Romero, two weeks before he was murdered for speaking about what pleases God, said:

> Martyrdom is a grace from God that I do not believe that I have earned. . . . May my death, if it is accepted by God, be for the liberation of my people. . . . You can tell them, if they succeed in killing me, that I pardon them. . . .

These and many others like them seem to have been brought by the grace of God and their relationship with Jesus to that point where they are already living the resurrected life of Jesus. With the risen Christ they live, as Sebastian Moore puts it, no longer "under the shadow of death", but "in the light with death behind" them. "The virus of eternity has entered" their "bloodstream forever" (*Christ the Liberator of Desire*).

These are examples of people who have found blessedness even in the most harrowing of circumstances by knowing and following what pleases God. But what of us ordinary folk who try to live a Christian life? Do we find happiness in knowing and doing what pleases God? I leave the answer to each of my readers. For myself I have to say what I said years ago when a group of Jesuits were arguing about the merits of living a religious life with vows of poverty, chastity and obedience. I became irritated with the utilitarian arguments for the religious life and blurted out something like this: "I believe that God wants me to be a Jesuit for my happiness and good, and I am very grateful to God for this." Now over thirty years later I can still say that I feel blessed that I know and am trying to do what pleases God. It seems to me that knowing and doing what pleases God is also what most pleases me at the deepest level of my being. Does that sound right to you?

Chapter 6

Gratitude: A Fundamental Christian Virtue

In an article I once suggested that there are some people too traumatized by early life crises to be able to shift the focus from themselves to others. Such people, I opined, would be incapable of entering the stage of the spiritual journey that is called discipleship or the following of Jesus. In Ignatian terms these would be people who could not move beyond the First Week of the *Spiritual Exercises*. I referred to the example of the man from whom the legion of demons had been driven. When he wanted to follow Jesus, Jesus denied his request, saying: "Go home to your friends, and tell them how much the Lord has done for you, and what mercy he has shown you" (Mk 5:18-19). These lines, for some readers, may raise the specter of a caste Christianity, another instance of a distinction between real Christians and the also-rans. Truth to tell, some of the rhetoric of the literature on vocations to priesthood and religious life gives the impression that there are two classes of Christians. In this meditation I want to address that issue. I suggest that gratitude is the appropriate attitude for any Christian, and that gratitude will keep any of us from taking a "holier-than-thou" stance toward others.

The man from whom the legion of demons was driven out did not ask to be possessed by demons. Down's syndrome children do not bring on their condition. Battered and sexually abused children cannot be blamed for being born into families where such things happen. Moreover, if we have escaped being afflicted in any of these ways, we cannot take credit for it. Whenever we see someone afflicted, the only appropriate response is sympathy for the one afflicted and the realization, "There but for the grace of God go I." Indeed, since we do not know the mind of God, perhaps the most appropriate response is just gratitude for life and all it brings without any comparison at all to anyone else. Who knows whether it is better to be born without Down's syndrome than with it? To be an incest victim or not? At the least I want to raise the question for reflection.

In her short tale "Revelation" Flannery O'Connor tells the story of a day in the life of a Southern lady, Mrs. Turpin. In the course of a visit to the doctor she has occasion to congratulate herself a number of times on her superiority to those she encounters in the office. At the end of the story she has some kind of attack during which she has a revelation. She sees a vast swinging bridge.

> Upon it a vast horde of souls were rumbling toward heaven. There were whole companies of white-trash, clean for the first time in their lives, and bands of black niggers in white robes, and battalions of freaks and lunatics shouting and clapping and leaping like frogs. And bringing up the end of the procession was a tribe of people whom she recognized at once as those who, like herself and Claud, had always had a little of everything and the God-given wit to use it right. . . . They were marching behind the others with great dignity, accountable as they had always been for good order and common sense and respectable behavior. They alone were on key. Yet she could see by their shocked and altered faces that even their virtues were being burned away.

Mrs. Turpin discovers in this revelation that all of us human beings are equal in the sight of God. I suppose that the "tribe of people" like herself and Claud became more and more grateful as "their virtues were being burned away." As they were transformed, I wonder whether they made any comparisons at all, even in their gratitude. Remember that the Pharisee prayed in comparative form: "God, I thank you that I am not like other people: thieves, rogues, adulterers, or even like this tax collector. I fast twice a week; I give a tenth of all my income." The tax collector to whom he is compared by Jesus prays without comparison: "God, be merciful to me, a sinner" (Lk 18:11-13).

Another example from literature may help to make the point. In *Franny and Zooey*, J. D. Salinger describes a conversation in the bathroom between Zooey and his mother. In the course of it his mother wonders whether Franny, Zooey's sister, needs to see a psychoanalyst. Zooey gets serious and says:

> For a psychoanalyst to be any good with Franny at all, he'd have to be a pretty peculiar type. I don't know. He'd have to believe that it was through the grace of God that he'd been inspired to study psychoanalysis in the first place. He'd have to believe that it was through the grace of God that he wasn't run over by a goddam truck before he ever even got his license to practice. He'd have to believe that it's through the grace of God that he has the native intelligence to be able to help his goddam patients at *all*. I don't know any *good* analysts who think along those lines. But that's the only kind of psychoanalyst who might be able to do Franny any good at all.

The kind of psychoanalyst Zooey describes is the kind of Christian Jesus wants as his follower and companion. Such a Christian will not easily mistake the gifts he or she has received as merit badges for honor and a higher place in the esteem of God or anyone else.

In the parable of the sower and the seed (Mt 13:1-9) Jesus speaks of the seed that fell on good soil and produced a crop. Notice that the crop produced can be a hundred, sixty or thirty times what was sown. In his explanation of the parable Jesus does not assign any negative connotation to the differences in yield in the good soil. No matter what the yield, "what was sown on good soil, this is the one who hears the word and understands it" (v. 23). According to this parable all we need to do is to open our hearts to the grace of God and let God take care of what harvest will be produced. Our gifts and talents may differ and as a result the harvest produced will differ. But such differences do not make some people better in the eyes of God. Whatever talents or gifts we have are just that, gifts. And gratitude is the only proper response to the reception of gifts.

The attitude of gratitude for talents runs counter to the competitive nature of our culture. From infancy we are taught to compare ourselves with others in terms of talent or looks. IQ tests, SAT scores, class rankings—all compel us to compare ourselves with others. In a culture such as ours the inability to do what others can do and are applauded for can lead to a sense of inferiority. Hence, the man from whom the legion of demons has been cast out would, in our country, tend to think of himself as less valued by Jesus than the apostles who get to follow him. Moreover, those who can easily do what is applauded and appreciated can come to consider the applause as deserved. It is relatively easy to pick up the attitude of the Pharisee in the gospel parable. Under these circumstances the Christian attitude of gratitude and of acceptance of the gifts one has does not come easily. We need to pray regularly and often for gratitude to God for who we are.

Perhaps, even more important is to pray to know in our bones that we are the apple of God's eye just as we are. Once a retreatant felt that Jesus was telling him: "I love no one more than I love you; but I don't love you more than anyone else."

This was a very consoling experience for him and left him feeling very grateful. Moreover, he had no basis for making comparative judgments about his worth in the eyes of Jesus. What a great relief and freedom it would be if we could believe in our bones that Jesus makes no comparisons, but loves each of us as we are, and wants the best for each of us.

If we are given this grace, then we will also be rid of the kinds of feelings of inferiority that lead to envy, comparative judgments, and a sense that the call of some people to follow Jesus radically as apostles makes them better Christians. St. Paul must have had such a grace and then realized how free it made him. Hence, he could insist so strongly that no one can boast except in the cross of Christ, that all of us are parts of the one body of Christ, that each of us needs to play our role in the building up of the body.

> But God has so arranged the body, giving the greater honor to the inferior member, that there be no dissension within the body, but the members may have the same care for one another. If one member suffers, all suffer together with it; if one member is honored, all rejoice together with it.
>
> Now you are the body of Christ and individually members of it. And God has appointed in the church first apostles, second prophets, third teachers; then deeds of power, then gifts of healing, forms of assistance, forms of leadership, various kinds of tongues. Are all apostles? Are all prophets? Are all teachers? Do all work miracles? Do all possess gifts of healing? Do all speak in tongues? Do all interpret? But strive for the greater gifts (1 Cor 12:24-30).

As we all know, Paul then swings into his famous hymn to love. Gratitude for the gift of who we are and have become by the grace of God does lead quite naturally into love.

Part 2

Paradoxes

Chapter 7

Be Not Afraid

Fear sits deep within each one of us. We are afraid of so many things, the dark, the discovery of our secret fault or "flaw," sickness, pain, loss of money or prestige or reputation, loss of our loved ones, death itself. Fear keeps us from trusting other people, from trying new things, even from enjoying life. I venture to say that fear may be *the* manifestation of original sin in our lives. Because of fear we find it very difficult to live out the dream of God for our universe, that it be a place where all people would live in harmony with the perfect community which is the triune God and with one another. Could it be that "it is a huge nothing that we fear?" In this short meditation I want to explore that question.

Seamus Heaney, in his poem entitled "Storm on an Island," from *Death of a Naturalist*, sets the stage.

> We are prepared: we build our houses squat,
> Sink walls in rock and roof them with good slate.
> This wizened earth has never troubled us
> With hay, so, as you see, there are no stacks
> Or stooks that can be lost. Nor are there trees
> Which might prove company when it blows full
> Blast: you know what I mean—leaves and branches
> Can raise a tragic chorus in a gale
> So that you listen to the thing you fear
> Forgetting that it pummels your house too.

But there are no trees, no natural shelter.
You might think that the sea is company,
Exploding comfortably down on the cliffs
But no: when it begins, the flung spray hits
The very windows, spits like a tame cat
Turned savage. We just sit tight while wind dives
And strafes invisibly. Space is a salvo,
We are bombarded by the empty air.
Strange, it is a huge nothing that we fear.

On the face of it, it seems, it is a huge *something* that we fear. The Aran Island folk have good reason to fear the storms that regularly beat upon them. It would be foolhardy not to fear the power of such storms. It is right for parents to teach their children to fear fire and bare electric wires, oncoming traffic, vicious dogs. Given the daily headlines in the newspapers, they have good reason to instill in their children a healthy fear of strangers, especially if they offer them rides. It is only sensible to be afraid of the loss of all means of support for oneself and one's family. Dire poverty, debilitating sickness, cruel suffering, are not things to be embraced as great boons. And death does deprive us of the refreshing and consoling presence of our loved ones. It does appear that Seamus Heaney has overstated his case in this poem.

And yet, a good case can be made for the contention that Jesus considered fear the opposite of faith, that he, therefore, would have agreed with Heaney. In the gospels Jesus does not equate lack of faith with failure to believe in doctrine. In the Sermon on the Mount he tells us not to worry about what we will eat or drink or how we will clothe ourselves. Those who do so worry are people "of little faith" (Mt 6:30). When the disciples rouse Jesus during the storm at sea, he says, "Why are you afraid? Have you still no faith?" (Mk 4:40). In another storm at sea Jesus comes to the disciples walking on the water. Again his message is "Don't be afraid." When Peter begins to walk on the water toward Jesus, fear takes over and he begins to sink. Jesus saves him and then asks: "You of little faith, why did you doubt?" (Mt 14:25-31). When Jesus tells the disciples that they will be flogged and arrested, he adds, "When they hand you over, do not worry about how to speak or what you are to say; for what you are to say will be given to you at that time; for it is not you who speak, but the Spirit of your Father speaking through you" (Mt 10: 19-20), and later, "So do not be afraid; you are of more value than many sparrows" (v. 31). From this sampling of Jesus' words we can draw the conclusion that the opposite of faith is fear, that fear and faith are incompatible.

In these passages Jesus faces the disciples with many of the common fears of the human race. We fear that there will not be enough of the goods of this world to go around and that we will go hungry or thirsty or unclothed. We fear the unknown and so tend to avoid anything new or unexpected. We fear the loss of our reputations or our good name if we take a stand for what is right against the weight of public opinion. We fear, above all, pain, suffering and death. Jesus tells us that all these fears reveal our lack of faith.

But we return to the earlier consideration. To fear penury, loss of our good name or arrest and death seems only reasonable. No sensible person would, for example, give up his or her health or life insurance. And isn't the provision of such insurance precisely to keep fear at bay? Does the faith Jesus demands mean that the things we take for granted, like job security and tenure requirements, social security, health and life insurance, savings for a rainy day, are to be relinquished? At one point in the gospel when Jesus said how hard it was for a rich person to enter the kingdom of heaven, the disciples asked in amazement, "Then who can be saved?" (Mt 19:25). We may feel the same amazement.

Jesus' answer at that time may point us in a more hopeful direction. "For mortals it is impossible, but for God all things are possible" (v. 26). Apparently, God can make up for our lack of faith and thus bring us home safely to the kingdom in spite of the fears that bind us. I would also say that the use of the various kinds of insurance is not at issue; rather the problem comes when we put all our reliance on them so that we become paralyzed by fear at the thought of losing any of these perquisites of our society. The parable of the rich fool can help us here (Lk 12:13-21). He tears down his barns in order to build bigger ones to store all his grain and goods. This action does not seem to merit his condemnation, but rather the fact that he now relies on his stored goods without giving a thought to his mortality. The issue is not whether we have social security or job security, but whether we put our trust in these frail treasures to the point where we are paralyzed by fear when they are threatened.

These reflections take us in the direction of looking at what happens when we do put our trust in the security measures we have taken for ourselves and our loved ones. The story of the rich young man can serve as an illustration. He was a good man, one who had kept all the commandments.

> Jesus, looking at him, loved him and said, "You lack one thing; go, sell what you own and give the money to the poor, and you will have treasure in heaven; then come, follow me." When he heard this, he was shocked and went away grieving, for he had many possessions (Mk 10:21-22).

The poignancy in the story comes in the last line, he "went away grieving." Because of his inordinate attachment to his wealth he cannot have what he really wants, close companionship with Jesus. When we put too much of our hopes on security measures, on reputation, on wealth, on our degrees, we cannot really be happy. Worse yet, we cannot enjoy the very things we covet so much because we fear their loss so much. Think of the jealous lover who constantly agonizes about whether the beloved reciprocates his love.

Have you ever noticed the faces of people and noted the ones that radiated an inner happiness and peace? Aren't they the people who are not attached inordinately to what they

have or to what they have achieved? Near the end of his life
Ignatius of Loyola was described as full of life and radiating
an inner joy. One reason for the inner joy could have been his
lack of fear of the loss of anything he held dear. He told one
companion that if the pope should dissolve the Society of
Jesus it would take him only fifteen minutes to attain serenity.
In his *Autobiography* he also says that in his last years the
thought of his impending death gave him such joy that he
dissolved in tears. Obviously he loved the Society and his
life, but he had been brought by grace to the point where he
was not inordinately attached to either of them. And so, he
was an eminently happy man.

Pedro Arrupe, the late Father General of the Jesuits, tells
the story of celebrating Mass in one of the poorest slums of a
city in Latin America.

> The Mass was held in a small, open building in very
> poor repair; there was no door, and dogs came and
> went freely. Mass began with hymns accompanied by
> a guitarist, and the result was marvelous. The words
> of the hymn went: "Love is giving of oneself, forget-
> ting oneself, while seeking what will make others
> happy. . . ." As the hymn continued I felt a lump in
> my throat. I had to make a real effort to continue the
> Mass. These people seemed to possess nothing and
> yet they were ready to give of themselves to com-
> municate joy and happiness.

He then says that a big man invited him to come to his
place. At first Pedro was reluctant to accept, but encouraged
by one of the priests, he went. The man's place was a hovel
ready to collapse.

> He had me sit down on a rickety old chair. From there
> I could see the sunset. The big man said to me, "Look,
> sir, how beautiful it is!" We sat in silence for several
> minutes. The sun disappeared. The man then said, "I
> don't know how to thank you for all you have done
> for us. I have nothing to give you, but I thought you

would like to see this sunset. You liked it, didn't you? Good evening."

Every time I read this story, a lump comes to my throat and tears to my eyes. Here is a man who really is poor in spirit and is blessed.

Perhaps, after all, it is "a huge nothingness that we fear." Perhaps the only way that we can really enjoy what we have is not to fear its loss. And that includes health, vitality, the goods of this world, friends, life itself. In the Principle and Foundation of the *Spiritual Exercises* Ignatius indicates that a profound experience of God as the only true satisfaction of our deepest desires can lead us to what he calls indifference toward all other things. One translation of "indifference" is "being at a balance toward," or "not being inordinately attached to" all other things. As previously noted, this experience of the desire for God or for "we know not what" is what C. S. Lewis calls joy, a desire which is more fulfilling and delightful than the possession of any other good. In thrall to this desire we will be able, as Ignatius puts it, not "to prefer health to sickness, riches to poverty, honor to dishonor, a long life to a short life." We only want "what is more conducive to the end for which we are created," which is union with the triune God. Perhaps, then, the beatitudes are the truest of all the sayings of Jesus because only those who love God more than anything else can be truly blessed. But only those who have the faith Jesus spoke of, the faith which is the opposite of fear, can really say and mean, "Blessed are the poor in spirit . . . Blessed are those who mourn . . . Blessed are the meek . . . Blessed are those who are persecuted because of righteousness. . . ."

Of course, none of us can, by willing it, attain the "indifference" that is a prerequisite to blessedness. Our hearts, at their most profound levels, may desire union with the triune God, but we also know that at other levels they desire many other things and these desires are not usually ordered, but disordered and inordinate. What can we do to attain true happiness? We can beg God to help us to get our hearts in order; we can pay attention to our inner movements and begin to discern which of these movements are for our peace. In other words, we can learn by trial and error and the grace of God what we really and most profoundly want and take the steps that will lead us in that direction. The *Spiritual Exercises* of Ignatius are one means to this blessed end. At any rate, if we want to be blessed, if we want to enjoy life and the goods of this life in any meaningful way, we need to come to believe deep in our hearts that "it is a huge nothing that we fear."

Chapter 8

"Take Heart, It Is I;
Do Not Be Afraid"

Recently I spent some time watching a goose family, parents and five goslings. I was making my annual retreat at Miramar Retreat Center, Duxbury, Massachusetts. The goslings were already rather well formed, but their necks had not yet reached the adult stage where they could stretch them out to watch all around. As I got to know their habits, I realized that they did not have to be on the alert. Wherever they went, one of the parents was in the lead, for the most part keeping an eye out for what lay ahead. The other parent usually walked behind, its neck extended to its full length, seemingly alert for danger from any side or behind. Whenever the family was feeding on the grass, one of the adults seemed to stand guard with its neck extended. It took some time of observing them to become aware of this pattern and some more time to make a connection. The goslings did not have to be afraid because they were always under the protection of their parents. Is it possible that this family of geese could teach us a lesson about how we might live life without being overcome by fear? I believe that reflection on this family of geese may help us not to be so afraid.

Of course, we might object that these goslings are too dumb to be afraid. All they want is to fill their bellies, and the means are at hand. So they go their merry way, just munching away, without a care in the world. And truth to tell, they did not seem to have much of a care for the most part. But I noticed that whenever one or the other got too far behind the lead parent (presumably the mother), he or she would flap wings and speed it up to catch up with the crowd. I got the impression that they were aware of the presence of the parents, especially of the one who led them. When that presence seemed to be gone, then, I felt, they showed some fear and did what they could to get back to the safety of the parents' presence. When Jesus wanted to encourage his disciples not to be afraid, he said: "Look at the birds of the air; they neither sow nor reap nor gather into barns, and yet your heavenly Father feeds them. Are you not of more value than they?" (Mt 6:26). Perhaps our goose family, birds mostly of the ground and the water, can help us to further deepen Jesus' analogy.

The goslings seem to be afraid only when they are not aware of the presence of the parents. In the gospels there are two different versions of the storm at sea. In Luke, Jesus is in the boat, but asleep, when the storm hits. The disciples are terrified and wake Jesus up, and he calms the storm (Lk 8:22-25). In Mark (and in Matthew) the disciples are alone in the boat during the storm and suddenly see Jesus coming toward them walking on the waters. They think it is a ghost and are terrified. Then Jesus says: "Take heart, it is I; do not be afraid" (Mk 6:50). The disciples are terrified because Jesus seems absent. Are they not like the goslings when they become aware of the absence of their parents? But in the presence of Jesus there is nothing to fear. Indeed, that seems to be the message Jesus tries to inculcate in them. "I am here; don't be afraid." Do we have similar experiences? I can say for myself that my anxieties and fears usually run rampant when I am out of touch with the presence of Jesus, of the Father or of the Holy Spirit.

Sometimes, thank God rarely, I cannot sleep. Usually it is because something is bothering me, and I cannot get it off my mind. I try to rationalize it away: "No one noticed that *faux pas* anyway." I get into imaginary conversations in which I explain how I was in the right and the other person in the wrong. I try to think of something else. Nothing works and so I toss and turn in fear and anxiety. At these moments I try to put my trust in God, but even that does not work. Sometimes exhaustion sets in, and I sleep fitfully. When I reflect on these times, I realize that even my "prayer" is somewhat desperate and that I do not have a felt sense of the presence of God. More recently I have found that trying to tell God how I feel, even when I do not have a sense of God's presence, gradually begins to help. I begin to quiet down and recognize that I am making a mountain out of a mole hill, that in the large scheme of things what I am worrying about is "small change," as it were. "Take heart, it is I; do not be afraid." Like the goslings in the presence of their parents, I have been freed of fear by the felt presence of Jesus, of God the Father/Mother, of the Holy Spirit.

Now this experience does not automatically make everything better thereafter. I believe that we have to cultivate a sense of the presence of God in our daily lives to be able to live without being controlled by fear. We cannot control our fears in healthy ways by dint of willpower, by willing ourselves to believe in God's presence. We need to experience that presence in a profound way. Like the goslings the felt presence needs to become second nature to us. Here I can only suggest that it takes practice on our part, practice in paying attention to God's presence in our daily lives. I suppose that anyone who reads a book like this one is into such practice, tries to become aware of the presence of God. I suggest that trying too hard to become aware of the presence of God may be counterproductive. It might be more conducive to a growing awareness of that presence to take a few moments each day to reflect on the past day to see when we were most alive and living in the present moment, when we were not worrying about the past or the future, but just alert to the present. In these moments, I believe, we are aware of the mystery of the moment and of the mysterious Stranger who makes our hearts burn within us (cf. Lk 24:32). Often, too, when we are anxious and feeling lost, we can allow the Lord to touch us with his calming presence by doing something "contemplative," like smelling the coffee or a rose, watching the sun on a tree or a family of geese, listening to music or to birds, feeling the breeze. Such contemplative activities allow the Spirit to make her presence felt.

Now it may be argued that the goslings are living in a dream world if they believe that staying in the presence of their parents will shield them from all harm. They could be shot by a hunter, snared by a hawk, poisoned by herbicides; the presence of their parents will not keep them from all harm. True enough; and we could say the same about our own confidence and peace in the presence of God. Trust in God's presence will not keep us from being mugged on city streets, from contracting cancer, from illness and bereavement and death. Jesus' trust in God did not prevent him from being tortured and horribly crucified. Here again, the goslings may tell us something. Suppose that the goslings were aware of the possibilities of sudden and painful suffering and death in spite of the presence of their parents. What good would it do to worry about these possibilities? Such worry would do nothing but spoil the enjoyment in what they had in the presence of their parents. So too, if we worry about all the bad things that could happen to us and try to shield ourselves at all costs against such eventualities, then we will live always in fear, and that is hell indeed. When Jesus says to his disciples, "Take heart, it is I; do not be afraid," he is not guaranteeing that they will never suffer, never die, only that he will be with them—and us. For those who have experienced that presence, that may be enough, indeed more than enough. Let me end with a wonderful aphorism of John

Macmurray which I cite often in my writing and repeat even more to myself.

> All religion . . . is concerned to overcome fear. We can distinguish real religion from unreal by contrasting their formulae for dealing with negative motivation. The maxim of illusory religion runs: "Fear not; trust in God and God will see that none of the things you fear will happen to you"; that of real religion, on the contrary, is "Fear not; the things that you are afraid of are quite likely to happen to you, but they are nothing to be afraid of" (*Persons in Relation*, p. 171).

Chapter 9

Appearance and Reality

Pilate: "So you are a king?"
Jesus: "You say that I am a king" (Jn 18:37).

We have heard these words so often that we may not advert to the incongruity. Jesus had been arrested the evening before and brought before the Sanhedrin where he was accused of crimes worthy of death. He might have had a black eye from the blow to the face he received from one of the servants of the High Priest. He has been up all night, part of the time being made sport of by the guards. His clothes might have been torn and dirty and covered with spittle and spots of his own blood. He probably smelled bad. One way to read Pilate's words is as an astonished: "*You*, a king? You look more like a common criminal or a bum." The only time in Jesus' life when it would have been more incongruous to call him a king would have been on the cross itself. Yet, at this nadir of his fortunes Jesus asserts quite openly, "Yes, I am a king."

Earlier in John's gospel when Jesus had fed the five thousand, Jesus had withdrawn to a mountain by himself when he "realized that they were about to come and take him by force to make him king" (Jn 6:15). By any standard we know, that was the moment to admit that he was a king. Not now when his friends are scattered, when one of his closest followers has betrayed him and another denied him three times. Yet he does not claim that he is a king when he is on top, but rather when he has hit rock bottom. There is something to ponder here.

Jesus, we believe, is *the* revelation of who God is and what God values. That revelation reaches its climax in the crucifixion and resurrection of Jesus. So Jesus' claim to kingship at this nadir of his earthly power says something about God as well as about Jesus. Yes, for God appearance and reality are topsy-turvy. The ones with the power—Annas and Caiaphas, Herod, Pilate—have nothing that God holds dear or that would make them kings in God's eyes whereas the one with no power, the one who has been handed over to the powerful ones, has. Indeed, Christian artists have always known that Jesus dying on the cross as a common criminal is God's version of what a king is and should be. This beaten, bruised young man, torn and bleeding, crowned with thorns, horribly wracked by thirst and pain, is the Savior of the world, the long-awaited Messiah, God's king.

Pondering the paradox of the scene at Pilate's palace should shake up some of our deeply ingrained presuppositions and prejudices, but only if we let the message of that scene sink in. We are, after all, conditioned by our culture to judge by appearances. Why else are we so shocked by revelations of child abuse among the affluent and almost take it for granted among the poor? Why else do we assume that the children of the well-to-do will be academically bright while those of the poor and of minorities will be academically slow? Crime in run-down neighborhoods of our inner cities is expected; it is news when it occurs in upper-class neighborhoods. The shock value of the parable of the Good Samaritan rests on the assumptions and prejudices of Jesus' audience. The priest and the levite are expected to act charitably toward the wounded man. No one in Jesus' audience would expect such behavior from a despised Samaritan. To bring home the parable to us we would have to change the Samaritan into a member of the most despised and disregarded group we know. Is it not true that we are genuinely surprised by kindness and charity shown to us by someone of a different race and social class? Much in our culture teaches us to esteem and expect more of people who are white, well dressed, well heeled, and who speak English in a cultured way. We look up to those who have power and esteem. (I am rather amazed at the change in attitude that comes over people when they hear that I am a provincial, as though having that job automatically makes me a better person.) We do tend to judge by appearances. We do not, from our culture, imbibe God's values. We need to let the horror of the crucifixion shock us into the realization that we do not judge as God does.

In his inimitable style Frederick Buechner contrasts appearances and reality from the point of view of the gospels.

> In the world of the fairy tale, the wicked sisters are dressed as if for a Palm Beach wedding, and in the world of the Gospel it is the killjoys, the phonies, the nitpickers, the holier-than-thous, the loveless and cheerless and irrelevant who more often than not wear the fancy clothes and go riding around in sleek little European jobs marked Pharisee, Corps Diplomatique, Legislature, Clergy. It is the ravening wolves who wear sheep's clothing. And the good ones, the potentially good anyway, the ones who stand a chance of being saved by God because they know they don't stand a chance of being saved by anybody else? They go around looking like the town whore, the village drunk, the crook from the IRS, because that is who they are. . . .
>
> And as for king of the kingdom himself, whoever would recognize him? He has no form or comeliness. . . . He smells of mortality. We have romanticized his raggedness so long that we can catch echoes only of

the way it must have scandalized his time in the horrified question of the Baptist's disciples, "Are *you* he who is to come?" (Mt 11:13); in Pilate's "Are you the king of the Jews?" (Mt 27:11) (*Telling the Truth: The Gospel as Tragedy, Comedy and Fairy Tale*).

To become a member of most organizations one has to have some positive quality. To become a member of Mensa a person must prove that his or her IQ is at least 140. To get into a university one needs a diploma from a proper school. To become a member of the Medical Association one must have graduated from a medical school. One of my friends once noted that it does not work this way with the organization called Alcoholics Anonymous. To become a member of AA one need only stand up in a meeting and say: "I'm Joe, and I'm an alcoholic." Many people are deterred from getting the help they need because they are ashamed to make this statement. Appearances get in the way of reality. The reality is that most people react with admiration when someone admits the truth that will set him or her free. My friend then went on to note that the entrance card for membership in the Christian church is similar to that of AA. One need only say: "I'm Joe and I'm a sinner in need of salvation." Again many find it difficult to admit their reality and hide behind appearances, thus depriving themselves of saving grace, freedom and a path to true happiness. The parable of the prodigal son illustrates God's view of reality. There the father embraces with love and happiness his son who admits that he is a sinner in need of forgiveness. To enter into a more intimate relationship with God we need no other qualification than the willingness to admit the truth about ourselves. But because of our conditioning we find it quite difficult to admit the truth and thus move toward freedom and joy, the kind of freedom and joy described by Hopkins at the end of his "Heraclitean Fire" poem:

In a flash, at a trumpet crash,
I am all at once what Christ is, since he was
    what I am, and
This Jack, joke, poor potsherd, patch, matchwood,
    immortal diamond,
Is immortal diamond.

In following Jesus as disciples our presuppositions and prejudices also get in the way, just as they got in the way of the disciples. In Mark's gospel Jesus predicts his imminent crucifixion and death, and each time the disciples miss the message because they are blinded by their own presuppositions about what kind of Messiah would come. After the first prediction Peter in horror takes him aside and begins to rebuke him. After the second the disciples get into an argument as to which of them was the greatest. After the third James and John approach Jesus and ask to be able to sit at his right and left in his kingdom. When the other disciples hear of this, they become indignant. Those of us who want to become Jesus' disciples in our own age can be blinded just as easily.

In *The Brothers Karamazov* Dostoevsky has Ivan tell the story of the Grand Inquisitor in which Jesus is once again killed, but this time by the leaders of the Catholic Church in Spain at the time of the Inquisition. If Jesus were to reappear in our midst, would he fare any better than he did in Roman-occupied Israel? We have some evidence of how he would be treated in the way those who follow him unreservedly are treated. The kind of honesty and willingness to face reality that got Jesus killed can infect those who get close to him now and get them killed. Witness Oscar Romero. Witness the thousands of catechists in Central and South America who have been killed because they preached the gospel. Witness the Jesuits at the University of Central America in El Salvador who were slaughtered along with their cook and her daughter because they told the truth. These and many other cruel murders testify to the fact that our "Christian" world still judges differently than does God about reality.

Moreover, we may resist getting close to Jesus because we fear the consequences for our lifestyle. In the last meditation we pondered the story of the rich young man whose attachment to his great wealth kept him from following Jesus. He went away grieving. The sad aspect to this story is that the young man loses what he most wants because of the illusion that he could not do without what his wealth could bring him. The reality is that his own deepest happiness lay in following his heart's desire which was to be with Jesus. Again we see that appearances get in the way of seeing reality.

We come back to Jesus facing Pilate and his own death by crucifixion. In this dark hour Jesus reveals what is at the heart of reality. It is a self-sacrificing God, a God who embraces what is most antithetical to God, namely death and evil, and makes them part of who God is. After this dark hour anyone who contemplates Jesus sees God in a human body with the wounds of the crucifixion in his hands, feet and side. As he stood before Pilate and hung on the cross at Golgotha appearances would say that Jesus was a total failure. Appearances were that he had not brought about the conversion of his people. Indeed, if this "worm and no man" was the Messiah, then God had perpetrated a cruel hoax on his people. Lying, cowardly kowtowing to Roman authority and cruelty and naked power had prevailed. On the cross Jesus was mocked and ridiculed; and if he is God, then God was mocked and ridiculed. Evil seems to have triumphed. It is hard to imagine anything more antithetical to God than the unspeakable horrors that are visited on this innocent human being. Yet the reality is that Jesus is a king; Jesus so horribly tortured is God incarnate, is "the power of God and the wisdom of God" (1 Cor 1:24). The powers of darkness and the evil that lurks in the hearts of human beings have their day and seem to win. But

Jesus, the power and wisdom of God, and God himself let them have their way, embraced what they had to do and, in the face of all that overpowering evil, could say, precisely because of his oneness with God, "Father, forgive them; for they do not know what they are doing" (Lk 23:34).

It will pay us to reflect over and over again on this mystery of Jesus, the suffering king. In creation God produces what is not God, namely our universe, and makes this universe necessary. God could not be creator without the existence of the universe. God, however, does not create out of necessity, but because of overflowing love. With the crucifixion this overflowing love surpasses all human grasp because now God bears in human flesh the results of appalling evil. To be the Christ (Messiah, Savior of the world, king) he now is, these wounds are necessary. "Was it not necessary that the Messiah should suffer these things and then enter into his glory?" (Lk 24:26). The appearances of powerlessness, of criminality, of absolute weakness are now the reality of God. As Paul says: "For the message about the cross is foolishness to those who are perishing, but to us who are being saved it is the power of God" (1 Cor 1:18).

In "God's Grandeur" Hopkins caught the difference between appearance and reality for those who believe in the kingship of the broken Jesus.

> The world is charged with the grandeur of God.
>   It will flame out, like shining from shook foil;
>   It gathers to a greatness, like the ooze of oil
> Crushed. Why do men then now not reck his rod?
> Generations have trod, have trod, have trod;
>   And all is seared with trade; bleared, smeared
>   with toil;
>   And wears man's smudge and shares man's
>   smell: the soil
> Is bare now, nor can foot feel, being shod.

And for all this, nature is never spent;
    There lives the dearest freshness deep
    down things;
And though the last lights off the black West went
    Oh, morning, at the brown brink eastward,
    springs—
Because the Holy Ghost over the bent
    World broods with warm breast and with ah!
    bright wings.

Chapter 10
Mysticism in Hell

The word mystic usually conjures up images of nuns wrapped in voluminous and flowing gowns swooning in ecstasy or of fierce ascetics of the desert, fighting off the devil's allures. Mystics are associated with cloisters, with vows of poverty and chastity, and with long hours of prayer in their monastery cells and in chapel.

What are we to make, then, of Etty Hillesum, the Dutch Jewess who died in Auschwitz on November 30, 1943? In her diary, published under the title *An Interrupted Life: The Diaries of Etty Hillesum 1941-43*, she says, knowing full well that arrest and transport await her, "For once you have begun to walk with God, you need only keep on walking with Him and all of life becomes one long stroll—such a marvelous feeling. . . . I hate nobody. I am not embittered. And once the love of mankind has germinated in you, it will grow without measure" (p. 189). These and other entries witness to a union with God that can only be called mystical. Yet Etty was no cloistered virgin. Her first entry says: "I am accomplished in bed, just about seasoned enough I should think to be counted among the better lovers, and love does indeed suit me to perfection, and yet it remains a mere trifle, set apart from what is truly essential, and deep inside me something is still locked away" (p. 1). Her diaries attest to a somewhat bohemian lifestyle far from monastic quiet. And of course, the menace of the Nazi occupiers permeates the atmosphere. Those of us who of necessity have to find God in the hurly-burly of an active lifestyle and in less than ideal personal circumstances may find encouragement from reflection on Etty's diaries.

Etty was born on January 15, 1914, one of three rather brilliant children born of the turbulent marriage between a Dutch Jewish schoolteacher and headmaster and a Russian Jewish mother. After leaving her father's school in 1932, Etty took her first degree in law at the University of Amsterdam and then enrolled in the department of Slavonic Languages. The diaries indicate that she earned some of her living expenses by tutoring in Russian. We do not know much of her life up to Sunday, March 9, 1941, when she made her first entry in her diaries. From the diaries we learn that her life revolved around two circles of people, one the group of five with whom she lived, the other a group of followers of a somewhat enigmatic and yet mesmerizing German Jew, Julius Spier.

The group of five was headed by a sixty-two-year-old widower, Han Wegerif who had invited Etty in as a sort of housekeeper. She soon became his lover. Etty met Spier in January, 1941, it seems, and also became his patient in a rather strange psychotherapy that included wrestling. After a few sessions she became his confidant and then his lover. Psychologists could have a field day analyzing Etty's trans-ference and Spier's countertransference. Yet through this relationship Etty found God. After Spier died in September, 1942, Etty addresses him in her diary: "You taught me to speak the name of God without embarrassment. You were the mediator between God and me, and now you, the mediator, have gone and my path leads straight to God. It is right that it should be so. And I shall be the mediator for any other soul I can reach" (pp. 209-10).

And near the end of the diaries, Etty writes:

And when the turmoil becomes too great and I am completely at my wits' end, then I still have my folded hands and bended knee. A posture that is not handed down from generation to generation with us Jews. I have had to learn it the hard way. It is my most precious inheritance from the man whose name I have almost forgotten but whose best part has become a constituent of my own life. What a strange story it really is, my story: the girl who could not kneel. Or its variation: the girl who learned to pray. That is my most intimate gesture, more intimate even than being with a man. After all one can't pour the whole of one's love out over a single man, can one? (p. 240).

Whatever else we can say about the therapeutic relationship between Etty and Spier—and Etty was not blind to Spier's weaknesses—he was the catalyst for a remarkable transformation in Etty Hillesum. In the course of the year and a half recorded in these diaries Etty develops from a young woman controlled by her moods and fears to a spiritually mature person who can fairly be described as a mystic in the hell created by the Nazis in occupied Europe. How did this transformation come about?

What strikes a reader immediately is her fierce candor about herself and her situation and her strong desire to be true to her God. In November, 1941, she notes that something has pulled her back to her roots, that as she cycled home the night before she babbled something like this:

God, take me by Your hand, I shall follow You dutifully, and not resist too much. I shall evade none of the tempests life has in store for me, I shall try to face it all as best I can. But now and then grant me a short respite. I shall never again assume, in my innocence, that any peace that comes my way will be eternal. I shall accept all the inevitable tumult and struggle. I delight in warmth and security, but I shall not rebel if I have to suffer cold, should You so decree. I shall follow wherever Your hand leads me and shall try not to be afraid. I shall try to spread some of my warmth, of my genuine love for others, wherever I go. But we shouldn't boast of our love for others. We cannot be sure that it really exists. I don't want to be anything special, I only want to try to be true to that in me which seeks to fulfil its promise. I sometimes imagine that I long for the seclusion of a nunnery. But I know that I must seek You amongst people, out in the world (pp. 64-65).

Along with the candor there seems to have developed a willingness to speak honestly to God. In April, 1942, she writes:

I am still assailed far too much by words like these [unflattering comments about her]. I prayed early this morning, "Lord, free me from all these petty vanities. They take up too much of my inner life and I know only too well that other things matter much more than being thought nice and charming by one's fellows." What I mean is: that sort of thing mustn't take up too much of your time and imagination. For then you get carried away with: "what a nice person I am, what fun I am, how much everyone must like me" (p. 120).

By the end of April her spiritual regimen of honesty and candor with herself and God leads to this assertion:

Instead of living an accidental life, you feel deep down that you have grown mature enough to accept your "destiny." Mature enough to take your "destiny" upon yourself. And that is the great change of the last year. I don't have to mess about with my thoughts any more or tinker with my life, for an organic process is at work. Something in me is growing and every time I look inside, something fresh has appeared and all I have to do is to accept it, to take it upon myself, to bear it forward and to let it flourish (p. 136).

On May 18, 1942, she writes about the growing threat and terror and then says: "I draw prayer round me like a dark protective wall, withdraw inside it as one might into a convent cell and then step outside again, calmer and stronger and more collected again" (p. 139). And just eight days later she can write this prayer:

> It is sometimes hard to take in and comprehend, oh God, what those created in Your likeness do to each other in these disjointed days. But I no longer shut myself away in my room, God, I try to look things straight in the face, even the worst crimes, and to discover the small, naked human being amidst the monstrous wreckage caused by man's senseless deeds. I don't sit here in my peaceful flower-filled room, praising You through Your poets and thinkers. That would be too simple, and in any case I am not as unworldly as my friends so kindly think. Every human being has his own reality, I know that, but I am no fanciful visionary, God, no schoolgirl with a "beautiful soul." I try to face up to Your world, God, not to escape from reality into beautiful dreams— though I believe that beautiful dreams can exist beside the most horrible reality—and I continue to praise Your creation, God, despite everything (pp. 140-41).

On June 19 she writes: "We try to save so much in life with a vague sort of mysticism. Mysticism must rest on crystal-clear honesty, can only come after things have been stripped down to their naked reality" (p. 149). The very next day she speaks of seeing more and more signs barring Jews from most paths and open country. Then she adds:

> But above the one narrow path still left to us stretches the sky, intact. They can't do anything to us, they really can't. They can harass us, they can rob us of our material goods, of our freedom of movement, but we ourselves forfeit our greatest assets by our misguided compliance. By our feelings of being persecuted,

humiliated and oppressed. By our own hatred. . . . We may of course be sad and depressed by what has been done to us; that is only human and understandable. However: our greatest injury is one we inflict upon ourselves. I find life beautiful and I feel free. The sky within me is as wide as the one stretching above my head. I believe in God and I believe in man and I say so without embarrassment. Life is hard, but that is no bad thing. . . . True peace will come only when every individual finds peace within himself; when we have all vanquished and transformed our hatred for our fellow human beings of whatever race—even into love one day, although perhaps that is asking too much. It is, however, the only solution. I am a happy person and I hold life dear indeed, in this year of Our Lord 1942, the umpteenth year of the war (p. 151).

As the certainty of the intention of the Nazis to exterminate all Jews grows in her, the willingness to confront reality also grows. In early July she writes:

Something has crystallized. I have looked our destruction, our miserable end which has already begun in so many small ways in our daily life, straight in the eye and accepted it into my life, and my love of life has not been diminished. I am not bitter or rebellious, or in any way discouraged. . . . I have come to terms with life. . . . By "coming to terms with life" I mean: the reality of death has become a definite part of my life; my life has, so to speak, been extended by death, by my looking death in the eye and accepting it, by accepting destruction as part of life and no longer wasting my energies on fear of death or the refusal to acknowledge its inevitability. It sounds paradoxical: by excluding death from our life we cannot live a full life, and by admitting death into our life we enlarge and enrich it (pp. 162-63).

As the diaries come to an end, one senses an ever-deepening conviction in her that no matter what happens—and she never shuts her eyes to the horrible fate in store for her and all Jews—God will sustain her. Indeed, she becomes more and more convinced that her mission in life is to accept into her heart the sufferings of others and not to respond with bitterness. When she does quaver before the enormity she faces, she pours out her heart to her God and finds peace. For example, here is a Sunday morning prayer in July:

> Dear God, these are anxious times. Tonight for the first time I lay in the dark with burning eyes as scene after scene of human suffering passed before me. I shall promise You one thing, God, just one very small thing: I shall never burden my today with cares about my tomorrow, although that takes some practice. Each day is sufficient unto itself. I shall try to help You, God, to stop my strength ebbing away, though I cannot vouch for it in advance. But one thing is becoming increasingly clear to me: that You cannot help us, that we must help You to help ourselves. And that is all we can manage these days and also all that really matters: that we safeguard that little piece of You, God, in ourselves. And perhaps in others as well. Alas, there doesn't seem to be much You Yourself can do about our circumstances, about our lives. Neither do I hold You responsible. You cannot help us but we must help You and defend Your dwelling place inside us to the last. . . . No one is in their clutches who is in Your arms. I am beginning to feel a little more peaceful, God, thanks to this conversation (p. 186-87).

These last words speak volumes about how Etty developed her relationship and point the way any one of us can take, namely, to pour out our hearts to God. But her conversations with God are not only about painful matters. Later on in this same prayer she recalls the jasmine tree behind her house which has been destroyed by storms, and then goes on to say to God:

87

But somewhere inside me the jasmine continues to blossom undisturbed, just as profusely and delicately as ever it did. And it spreads its scent round the House in which You dwell, oh God. You can see, I look after You, I bring You not only my tears and my forebodings on this stormy, grey Sunday morning, I even bring You scented jasmine. And I shall bring You all the flowers I shall meet on my way, and truly there are many of those. I shall try to make You at home always. Even if I should be locked up in a narrow cell and a cloud should drift past my small barred window, then I shall bring You that cloud, oh God, while there is still the strength in me to do so. I cannot promise You anything for tomorrow, but my intentions are good, You can see (p. 188).

Because of her inner transformation she desires to become "a center of peace in that madhouse" (the Jewish Council where she worked for a couple of weeks) and then the "thinking heart" of Westerbork camp. She is convinced that the world's only hope is for human beings to accept life with all its bitterness and suffering lovingly. And she conceives her own "apostolate" in this way:

How great are the needs of Your creatures on this earth, oh God. They sit there, talking quietly and quite unsuspecting, and suddenly their need erupts in all its nakedness. Then, there they are, bundles of human misery, desperate and unable to face life. And that's when my task begins. It is not enough simply to proclaim You, God, to commend You to the hearts of others. One must also clear the path towards You in them, God, and to do that one has to be a keen judge of the human soul. . . . I embark on a slow voyage of exploration with everyone who comes to me. And I thank You for the great gift of being able to read people. Sometimes they seem to me like houses with open doors. . . . And every one must be turned into a dwelling dedicated to You, oh God. And I promise

88

You, yes, I promise that I shall try to find a dwelling and a refuge for You in as many houses as possible (pp. 214-15).

Again in September she writes of her desires:

With a sharp pang, all of suffering mankind's nocturnal distress and loneliness passes now through my small heart. What shall I be taking upon myself this winter?
"One day, I would love to travel through all the world, oh God; I feel drawn right across all frontiers and feel a bond with all Your warring creatures." And I would like to proclaim that bond in a small, still voice but also compellingly and without pause. But first I must be present on every battlefront and at the center of all human suffering (p. 225).

Her diaries end with these words, "We should be willing to act as a balm for all wounds." Apparently Etty was willing.

These diaries give eloquent testimony that even in the hell of the "Final Solution," God was not absent, that relating to God openly and candidly can transform a person dramatically, and that we do not need to be very "pious" or even "religious" in the ordinary sense of the term to engage in the relationship. God, it seems, is ready to engage in a relationship with us whenever we want to begin. We do not even have to "get our act together" before we can begin to relate to God. Finally, those who help us on the way to God may be the least expected kind of people. In one of her letters from Westerbork camp the month before she was transported to Auschwitz she tells her friend Tide what she had just written in her diary: "You have made me so rich, oh God, please let me share out Your beauty with open hands" (p. 255). The preservation of these diaries was the answer to her prayer.

Chapter 11

The Inventiveness of God

Do you remember how you reacted when you first heard that heaven would consist of the beatific vision? "What's that?" you might have said in your head, if not out loud. Then it was explained that the beatific vision meant looking at and enjoying God for all eternity. Did you wonder whether you'd be bored, whether there might also be something else to do? Being polite before God, if you did have such thoughts, you were probably like me and kept them to yourself. After all, heaven was a long way off, and there were still a lot of interesting things to do and see here on earth. We could let heaven take care of itself, whatever the beatific vision might mean.

Maybe it's the aging process that I think along these lines. A couple of years ago I had an insight that made the thought of heaven a lot more intriguing than the idea of gawking at a throne forever. I had spent the month of January at Eastern Point Retreat House in Gloucester, Massachusetts, directing people on retreat. The insight was the culmination of a month of noticing things.

Every day without exception at least five or six of the thirty-day retreatants could be found in the dining room looking out to sea for over an hour through the picture windows as the sky brightened and the sun rose. Since some of them talked to me each day about their prayer, I found out that they were never bored. Each day brought something new. The cloud pattern varied endlessly and affected how the light of the sun was seen. Some days the sun had to break through a low-lying bank of fog; some days the sun itself never appeared, but yet the darkness dissipated. The light on the water also varied depending on the tide, the direction of the wind, the temperature, and the cloud patterns. Each day also brought new experiences of God as they watched the sun rise.

Gloucester teems with bird life. Just the gulls alone are worth the price of admission. They come in various shades of gray, white and black, and they seem to revel in soaring with the wind or sometimes in soaring against the wind so that they seem motionless. At times they congregate by the hundreds on the iced-over pond facing in one direction for long periods of time. Sandpipers often do the same thing on one leg, droves of them all facing in the same direction. They even hop on the one leg, as though the first one to use two legs loses whatever game they are playing. Both the pond and the cove also teem with ducks of all varieties, and the closer you look, the more variegated are their colors. Some of the greens you can see only in a certain light and up close. Later, back in the city, I noticed a similar phenomenon in an ordinary pigeon; it turned in the sunlight, and just for a moment I saw a beautiful greenish blue in the neck feathers.

It's fun watching the ducks dive under water and then waiting for them to surface, and realizing that the ones you see are the same ones who dove minutes before. Then there were the swans like little boats in the water. The original two at Eastern Point now seem to have expanded to at least ten. On the last two days of January I counted eight sailing serenely in Brace's Cove, and later two more at Rocky Neck. They are so stately and lovely to look at, but I also wanted to see them fly and land. Finally one day I saw one of them come in for a landing and was surprised at how graceful the landing was.

Of course, there are also land birds around, not as many as in summer, but still an amazing number. You hear them more often than you see them. The caws of the crows are everywhere, but I also heard one sound that intrigued me for a few days because I could not seem to find the source. Whenever I heard it, I only saw crows nearby, and thought that it was too melodious a sound to come from them. But sure enough, one day I heard the sound and saw it coming from a crow. Even they have a lovely sound at times.

Twice during the month we sighted seals on the rocks in the cove. The first time it was a rather little one and relatively far away, so that even the binoculars did not give much of a look. But on the last day of the thirty-day retreat I saw a large seal on a rock fairly close by. The tide was coming in and gradually washing over more and more of the rock. The seal raised its head and tail as each wave moved over the rock, then finally gave up its perch and slid into the sea.

Whenever someone contemplates making a thirty-day retreat for the first time, he or she wonders how the time will pass. "Will I be bored?" "How many books should I bring?" "How can I ever spend that much time in prayer?" These are some of the questions that run through the minds of prospective retreatants. Not unlike the kinds of questions we might ask about heaven, if we ever give heaven a thought. Once again during that January I found that the retreatants were only bored when they became resistant to God's presence and closeness. For the most part of their retreats they were eager to spend time in prayer because the periods of prayer were so interesting. They found that God was not boring as company, nor did they seem boring to God.

I have now directed almost one hundred people on thirty-day retreats and many more than that on eight-day retreats. As a director I see each person I direct each day of the retreat to talk about what happened in their prayer during the previous day. I find myself endlessly intrigued by the variety of experiences people have of God. Not only am I not bored, I

93

find myself eager to listen to each new person. In the case of experiences of the relationship with God it is clearly not true that "when you've seen one, you've seen them all." Part of my motivation for being a spiritual director springs from the endless variety and interest of people's experiences with God.

Perhaps you are beginning to see where these cumulative experiences are leading with regard to the opening question about the beatific vision, whatever that phrase may mean. One day it dawned on me that God's creation has intrigued us human beings since the beginning of time. We have never tired of looking, listening, smelling, touching, testing, figuring out, trying to understand, trying to control, trying to fathom the created universe. Curiosity impels a child to try to make sense of his or her world; the same kind of curiosity impels an astronomer to spend days at a telescope or poring over photos in order to understand the universe. Human beings have never been bored with the created universe except when they are depressed. There are always new things to discover, to learn, to sense. The mystery writer Jane Langton, in *Good and Dead*, notes that the minister Joe Bold has always been intrigued by details around him. In adulthood, he

> learned that these airy manifestations were metaphors, mystical pedagogical remarks by God, who never stopped talking in a language composed of the droplets in a cloud or the sap running up a tree, or the willful behavior of the elements of a dividing cell. It was a garrulous communication that never ceased, a gabble of molecules, a continuous proclamation by cobblestones and the bark of trees, by constellations of stars and by cracks in the sidewalk, an endless monologue of visual splendors.

Think of how many times you can listen to an intriguing piece of music or read a novel or poem and discover new wrinkles each time. These are human creations, and the human creator is only a pale image of the Creator of the universe. The poet Brendan Galvin said in an interview, "Some writers come to feel that the reason the world exists is so that we can write about it. That's occurred to me." We can paraphrase him, perhaps, by saying that the reason the world exists is so that we can live in it and in the living become enthralled not only by the world but by its creator and ours. It struck me that we would need an eternity to enjoy the inventiveness, the playfulness, the seriousness, the creativity, the simplicity and complexity of our God. Heaven, whatever it is, will not be boring.

Of course, there's no need to rush it, is there?

Part 3

Our Role in
God's World

Chapter 12

Does God Need Us?

The Lord speaks to Job: "Who has given to me, that I should repay him? Whatever is under the whole heaven is mine" (Jb 41:11).

This text seems to render the question in the title absurd. For the believer God is absolutely self-sufficient. The triune community that is Mystery itself is perfect and needs no one and nothing else. Indeed, if that community needed anyone or anything else to fulfill itself, God would not be God. So the first answer to the question "Does God need us?" has to be an emphatic "No." God does not create a universe and other persons out of need. Moreover, the romantic notion that God creates us because otherwise God would be lonely has to be seen as nonsense, and heretical nonsense at that. God creates the universe and us not because of need, but because of overflowing love. One can imagine the three Persons who are the one God saying to each other: "Our community life is so good; why don't we share it with others?" As Sebastian Moore (in *Let This Mind Be in You*) notes, our desire for someone or something is aroused by its existing beauty; but God's desire for a universe and for us brings both into existence. So God does not need us.

This doctrine has often been misused to make people feel useless before God. The very fact that God desires the universe and us into existence means that both the universe and we are desirable to God. I want to meditate with you in this chapter in such a way that we can give a positive, and orthodox, answer to the question of the title.

If God, freely and out of love, wants to be creator of the universe, what is needed? Obviously God must will the existence of the universe. But the universe in existence is also necessary if God is to be truly the Creator of the universe. If God wants to have a universe where human beings can be invited into the community life of the Trinity, then people who can receive the invitation and respond to it are necessary. Thus, there is a real sense in which God "needs" the universe and the persons in it, but only because God freely decides to become the Creator of the universe and to invite persons into the community life of the Trinity.

We can take the argument a step further. We Christians believe that God wants all persons to become part of the community life of the triune God. The kingdom of God which Jesus preached can be understood as God's intention for the universe, namely, that the universe be a place where all men and women live in communion with the Trinity and thus in harmony with one another and with the rest of the universe. God wants the whole human race to become one family with God. But family and friendship cannot be coerced; human beings must freely choose to accept God's invitation to live as brothers and sisters in the one family of God. Thus if God's intention is to be realized, people must hear the invitation and respond positively to it. Because God wants the kingdom of God to exist, God needs people who will hear the word and live it out. God "needs" hearers and doers of the word in order to be who God wants to be for us.

Recently I was reflecting on the confession of Peter at Caesarea Philippi. The scene seems central to the synoptic gospels. After this scene the die seems to have been cast as far as Jesus is concerned. He turns his face resolutely toward Jerusalem and also begins earnestly teaching his disciples what his mission will be. After this scene, for example, he predicts his passion and death three times. In the scene Jesus asks the disciples, "Who do people say that I am?" When they tell him what people are saying, he then asks, "But who do you say that I am?" Peter answers for all, "You are the Messiah" (cf. Mk 8:27-30). Often enough when we contemplate this scene, we focus on who Jesus is for us. And rightly so. But is it not possible to look at the scene from Jesus' point of view? Could it not be that Jesus needs the disciples' response in order to clarify his own growing sense of his identity and destiny? Let us ponder this possibility for a few moments.

How does anyone come to know who he or she is and what life-work he or she will do? Certainly part of the answer comes from internal processes. I reflect on what my desires are, my hopes and dreams. In prayer I may ask God to help me to know how I should best live out my life. I notice my attractions, the kinds of people and literature that fire my imagination. Mentally I try on roles and professions. I may even apprentice myself for a time to a few possible life works. But, unless I am a megalomaniac or a pure dreamer, I cannot really know my identity and my way of life without dialogue with others. No sane person establishes an identity and a way of life without dialogue with other people and with institutions. For example, in an extended retreat by myself I may come to the clear decision that I should become a Jesuit. But before I can really know that this discernment is correct—is, as Ignatius of Loyola would say, confirmed—I must be accepted by the Society of Jesus and then must submit myself to the long process of becoming a Jesuit through interaction with other Jesuits in formation. I would like to speculate that for Jesus this dialogue with the disciples was part of his coming to terms with his role in life and his destiny. Jesus, like any human being, could not establish his identity without the help of others. Looked at in this way, this scene

101

shows that Jesus needs the response of Peter to "confirm" his own sense of mission.

Many Christians contemplate this scene and in their imaginations hear Jesus say to them, "Who do you say that I am?" Most of us who do this focus on our response to Jesus, on what he means to us. "You are my savior, my friend, the one who died that I might live, etc." Is it at all reasonable to ask what Jesus' reaction to us is? Obviously Jesus is not now discerning who he is and what his mission is to be. So he does not need my response in order to confirm his own identity. But is there a way in which my recognition of Jesus as my savior and dearest friend affects Jesus and his mission? First, suppose that no one now living recognized Jesus as Savior and Messiah. Then, in effect, he would not be savior for anyone. Moreover, in our present world there would be no people who related meaningfully to Jesus and thus made him present in the world; there would be no human sacramental signs of Jesus in our world. Finally, even if Jesus is, by his very being as God and a human being, intimately related to our world and to all people as savior and redeemer, it would be almost impossible for anyone to know of this reality. In effect, Jesus would be absent from the world people know, and he would have no relevance for us. In other words, without people who recognize and proclaim Jesus for who he is and wants to be, Jesus would not be the one he wants to be in this world. Thus, Jesus must still be interested in our responses to the question, "Who do you say I am?" Jesus still needs people who recognize him and believe in him in order for him to fulfill his mission to our world. Our responses to Jesus must mean a great deal to Jesus. We are important to him. In a real sense he "needs" us.

Let us continue along this line of reflection. Wherever we live and work, we believe, Jesus is present as savior and redeemer, as brother of every human being we meet. But who makes his presence palpable? Is it not the person who believes in and loves Jesus? Since the resurrection Jesus has needed the hands of Christians to reach out to touch with love and sympathy whose who are suffering, the compassionate eyes of Christians to show his compassion, the hearts of Christians to demonstrate his love of people these Christians meet. In front of the Jesuit parish church of Christ the King in San Diego there is a statue of Christ. He has no hands. This is not the work of vandals, but the intent of the artist to illustrate that Jesus needs the hands of his followers now. Those who believe in and love Jesus are changed by the quality of that relationship; they act differently than they would if they did not believe in and love Jesus.

A story may illustrate my meaning. The writer Garson Kanin (in *The Atlantic*, March, 1964) recounts his visits to Felix Frankfurter, the famous justice of the Supreme Court. One day Frankfurter says:

> I have had a serious experience here. . . . You saw that nurse who went out a while ago? The tall, pretty, blond one? Audrée? We've been spending many hours here together, and I've had an opportunity to find out a great deal about her life. She is a devout Catholic. Look here. I have spent a good deal of energy attempting to avoid prejudice. But the dogma of the Catholic Church, or of any other denomination for that matter, has always put me off. Now this girl, this Audrée—I have never known generosity of such quality, or such rare kindness. Oh yes, far, far beyond duty. Overwhelming courtesy. And I have been asking questions, delving into the matter, trying to discover the wellspring of such superior behavior. Do you know what it turns out to be? Can you guess? Simply this — a practical application of her Catholicism. I've never known anyone who practiced a religion, whose everyday life is based upon a religion as much as this girl's is.

Audrée may never have known the impact her lived faith had, but she made Jesus a palpable presence in that hospital.

She supplied the hands Jesus needed there. So a real relationship with Jesus has an impact even when the person who has that relationship does not mention Jesus. I venture to say that Jesus needs people like Audrée in order to be who he wants to be for people like Felix Frankfurter.

Of course, those who believe in and love Jesus can also, when it is appropriate, speak openly of the one whom they love. People are looking for such honest and effective affirmation. Witness the success of the "sects" who, while presenting a somewhat truncated version of the "good news," still speak of the centrality of Jesus and his importance for our lives. Without truncating the gospel we can both speak of the centrality of Jesus to our own lives and also help others to speak of what Jesus means to them. I recall a married woman who wept openly when she realized that she could speak of her love of Jesus with a spiritual director and get some help with this central relationship of her life. Those of us who believe in and love Jesus should not downplay the power of personal witness of our faith and love.

We say that we believe in the resurrection of Jesus. That means, at the least, that Jesus can be experienced as a real comforting presence to those who suffer and who grieve. Does it not also mean that our loved ones who have died in Christ can also be experienced as somehow alive in Christ? The risen Jesus needs friends who have experienced his reality in their lives to spread the word so that others may also open their hearts to experience his reality in this world. Jesus can only with difficulty be the consoler he wants to be if we who believe in him and experience him as our friend and consoler do not witness to him.

If God can be found in all things, as Ignatian spirituality proposes, then those of us who take this spirituality seriously are "needed" by God to discover the presence of God in the mundane and ordinary details of our own lives. If we can do that for ourselves, then perhaps we will be more able to help others to discover "the dearest freshness deep down things

/ Because the Holy Ghost over the bent / World broods with warm breast and with ah! bright wings," as Hopkins puts it. God needs people who, like Hopkins, can point to the signs of hope and love in a world that often seems bereft of both and of God.

In the letter to the Romans Paul touched on our topic when he said:

> For there is no distinction between Jew and Greek; the same Lord is Lord of all and is generous to all who call on him. For, "everyone who calls on the name of the Lord shall be saved."
>
> But how are they to call on one in whom they have not believed? And how are they to believe in one of whom they have never heard? And how are they to hear without someone to proclaim him? And how are they to proclaim him unless they are sent? As it is written, "How beautiful are the feet of those who bring good news" (Rom 10: 12-15).

Out of love, not necessity, God is now in the position of depending on us for what God hopes for the world. We are important to, indeed needed by God. What divine condescension! What great love!

Chapter 13

The Kingdom of God:
What Role Do We Play?

Scripture scholars cringe when they hear Christians talk
about building up the kingdom of God. Only God builds up
the kingdom. One can argue that the kingdom of God can be
understood as God's one action which is this universe, an
action whose intention is to create an environment where all
persons can enter into God's very own community life. As
such the kingdom is both immanent in and transcendent to
the universe. Our task, then, is to attune our actions to the
one action of God, for only when we are in tune with God's
one action can we be fully satisfied. We do not build up the
kingdom of God; rather we discover it insofar as we discern
how to align our actions with the one action of God which is
the kingdom of God. We discover it, in other words, when
we live as brothers and sisters with the intention not to
exclude any person in principle from our community and
when we create the structures that make the universal community of all persons more possible. Recently in a session of
spiritual direction I had an insight about another role we can
play in the discovery of God's kingdom.

Christians believe that God is both transcendent to and
immanent in this world. That is, we believe that at every
moment of the world's existence God is mysteriously acting

to achieve his one intention for the world. Ignatian spirituality speaks of finding God in all things, which assumes that God is "in all things" in some mysterious way. Thus, in any situation God is present and active and, therefore, to be found.

But suppose that no one were aware of God's presence. I am reminded of the question: does a tree falling in the woods make a noise if there is no one there to hear it? An example may help. A family is gathered around a dying father in a hospital room. Christians believe that God is present there in some mysterious way. But no one of those present is aware of or expecting God's presence. As the family watches silently and mourns, each person experiences a variety of emotions from anguish and despair to a strange sense of peace. While the father slips further into a coma, some put their arms around one another, one or two hold his hand, all sense that, painful as it is, it is good to be here. Afterwards, if they talk about the experience with one another, they may speak of the sense of togetherness and peace they felt. But they probably will not pay much attention to it, and it will soon pass out of memory. God, we might say, has been actively present in this sad situation, but no one noticed. One result of not noticing might well be a return to their normal relationships which are mostly distant and even acrimonious. A chance for reconciliation and deeper communion has been lost for lack of awareness. Yet, in those moments as their father was dying, they experienced the kingdom of God, God's action inviting them to become consciously a community in union with the community of the Trinity.

Now let's introduce into the same scene a family member who is alert to the presence of God in our world. She, too, is grieving the impending loss of her father, but she also prays silently, asking God to take care of him and the family. She notices the change of mood as the family members begin to comfort one another and say good-bye to their father. She feels closer to all of them herself, even to two of her brothers from whom she has been estranged. Her heart fills with gratitude to God as she recognizes God's hand at work in the room. Later she rather shyly tells her brothers and sisters of her experience in the hospital room. They respond in kind, each one recounting his or her own reactions during their father's dying moments. As they talk, they become aware of a deeper bond between them and have a sense that their father is still with them just as, they now believe, God is with them.

What role do we Christians have in God's one action which is the kingdom of God? One role, at least, is to become aware of God's action in our daily lives and to witness to it. In other words, God needs us, not so much to bring about his kingdom as to notice its presence in our midst. Wherever in our world people who should be enemies become friends, wherever injured people forgive those who have injured them, wherever love and care for one another overcome fear of one another, wherever the hungry are fed, the thirsty given a cup a water, the naked clothed, the homeless housed, and prisoners are visited, wherever, in other words, a community that is in principle inclusive exists, there the kingdom of God is present, there God is bringing about his kingdom (cf. Mt 25:31-46). But God's active presence will be missed if no one notices it or witnesses to it. Of course, we can only notice God's active presence if we are alert for it, if, in other words, we believe in and expect that God will be actively present to our lives. The two disciples on the road to Emmaus did not expect to meet Jesus alive and well on their journey. As a result, even though their hearts were burning as they walked along with the stranger and listened to him, they did not recognize him until much later at the breaking of the bread (Lk 24:13-32). Our first task, then, is to ask God to help us to a practical belief in his active presence to us.

Then we must school ourselves to pay attention to our experience of life in order to discern the touch of God, or what Peter Berger calls the "rumor of angels," from all the other influences on our experience. Every human experience is multi-dimensional. There are physical, biological, psychological, sociological, and cultural influences on every experience. But for believers there is also a religious dimension to every experience since they believe that at every moment of existence human beings encounter God. Discernment seeks to distinguish within our experience what is of God from what is not of God. (We might add here that another influence on our experience is the Evil One. A friend recently noted that our culture is coming around to the belief that God is not dead, but has not yet come to believe in the existence of the devil in spite of the massive evidence in our century of unparalleled evil.) God needs people who take the time to notice his action in the world. That is, God needs people who believe in a practical way in his active presence in this world and take the steps to discover that active presence through prayer, paying attention to their experience, and discernment. To become such practical believers many Christians in our day have returned to the ancient practice of consulting a spiritual director regularly.

Finally, having discerned the active presence of God in the events of our daily lives, we need to be willing to witness to what we have seen and heard. "We declare to you what was from the beginning, what we have heard, what we have seen with our eyes, what we have looked at and touched with our hands, concerning the word of life" (1 Jn 1:1). We do not have to become a preacher as was the writer of the First Letter of John. Nor do we have to become streetcorner evangelists. But each of us who notices the active presence of God can learn ways of pointing to that presence. Such pointing will be tentative, to be sure, because we are fallible human beings. Perhaps all we need do is to take the chance of talking about our experience. At a recent meeting of Jesuits I felt close to tears of gratitude at the way the discussion was moving from a certain fractiousness and desolation toward reconciliation and real dialogue and future planning. I silently thanked

110

God. Normally I do not mention such experiences in public, but this time I did. I told the group what I had experienced and that I believed that we had experienced the active presence of God. No one laughed or asked me to defend my statement. I presumed that others, too, felt the finger of God in the proceedings.

A final word on our role in the kingdom of God. Even though we do not build up the kingdom of God, God's kingdom would not be attained at all if no one cooperated with God's intention of forming a community of people who share in God's own community life. We can only discern the presence of God's kingdom in our lives by trying to attune our own actions to the one action of God which is his kingdom on earth. In other words, we cannot discover or discern God's kingdom theoretically, but only in practice, indeed in the practice of trying, with God's grace, to attune our actions with God's one action. God is only encountered in the real world with all its complexities and conflicting claims and influences. If we try to attune our actions to the one action of God, we are privileged to be co-creators with God, Father, Son, and Holy Spirit, of the one community which is God's kingdom.

Chapter 14

Who Will Tell the Story?

The poet Brendan Kennelly has imagined a world where the story of Christmas is no longer told.

The story was not born with Robbie Cox
Nor with his father
Nor his father's father
But farther back than any could remember.

Cox told the story
Over twelve nights of Christmas.
It was the story
Made Christmas real.
When it was done
The new year was in,
Made authentic by the story.
The old year was dead,
Buried by the story.
The man endured,
Deepened by the story.

When Cox died
The story died.
Nobody had time
To learn the story.
Christmas shrivelled,
The old year was dust,
The new year nothing special,

So much time to be endured.
The people withered.
This withering hardly troubled them.
The story was a dead crow in a wet field,
An abandoned house, a rag on a bush,
A sick whisper in a dying room,
The shaking gash of an old man's mouth
Breaking like burnt paper
Into black ashes the wind scatters,
People fleeing from famine.
Nobody has ever heard of them.
Nobody will ever speak for them.

I know the emptiness
Spread by the story's death.
This emptiness is in the roads
And in the fields,
In men's eyes and children's voices,
In summer nights when stars
Play like rabbits behind Cox's house,
House of the story
That once lived on lips
Like starlings startled from a tree,
Exploding in a sky of revelation,
Deliberate and free.

(From *A Time for Voices* by Brendan Kennelly)

In this poem, we can feel the bleakness left behind with the death of the Christmas story. Now try to imagine what our world would be like without the story of God's passionate love for us. Imagine what it might be like for Jews, even relatively irreligious Jews, if the story of the Passover were no longer told as something that affects them now. What if they had no stories of how God had intervened in their history to save them because of his predilection for them? Wouldn't life be barren and hopeless indeed, especially after the history of their persecution which culminated in this century with the Holocaust? And yet, thank God, each year all over the world at seder suppers during Passover the story

114

of the way God brought them as a people out of Egypt is told and gives them hope to face the new year with its light and darkness. Moreover, the story is not told as an historical fact that is over and done with. No, it is told, the way Cox told the story of Christmas, in such a way that it presently affects those who hear it. At the seder supper the story is told as something that is occurring now, for the people now gathered around this festive table.

And faithful Jews gather daily to recall the saving deeds of Yahweh and to praise and thank God. In the novel *Inside, Outside*, Herman Wouk's hero has just described his bar mitzva as a boy of thirteen. He then goes on to say:

> The morning after my bar mitzva, I returned with Pop to the synagogue. What a contrast! Gloomy, silent, all but empty; down in front, Morris Elfenbein and a few old men putting on prayer shawls and phylacteries. . . .
>
> If Pop hadn't made the effort I'd have missed the whole point. Anybody can stage a big bar mitzva, given a bundle of money and a boy willing to put up with the drills for the sake of the wingding. The backbone of our religion—who knows, perhaps of all religions in this distracted age—is a stubborn handful in a nearly vacant house of worship, carrying it on for just one more working day; out of habit, loyalty, inertia, superstition, sentiment, or possibly true faith; who can be sure which? My father taught me that somber truth. It has stayed with me, so that I still haul myself to synagogues on weekdays, especially when it rains or snows and the minyan looks chancy.

Here the novelist captures the essence of true religion, that somehow or other the story continues to be told, that somehow or other the experience of God's saving desire and actions are told in our "distracted world." Without the faithful remnant telling the story and praising God there would be "emptiness . . . in the roads / And in the fields, / In men's

115

eyes and children's voices" of Jews throughout the world. Thank God that day after day, year after year, there are people for whom the story of God's love affair with his chosen people is an alive and palpable experience, so alive that they are willing to "haul" themselves to the synagogue on weekdays, especially on bad days when the minyan (ten) is chancy. Thank God, too, that millions of Jews yearly celebrate the story of the night of Passover as a present saving event in their lives. If no one were to tell the story, then God's saving acts would be lost in the dim past reaches of history. They would not affect people now, and the world would be a poorer place indeed.

Think of what it would be like for us Christians if no one told the story of the birth, life, death, and resurrection of Jesus any more. No one would hear the stories of Zechariah and Elizabeth, the old childless couple who, wonder of wonders, conceive and bear a child who will be the herald of the long-awaited Messiah. We would miss the sense of hope in God's goodness in spite of appearances which this story rouses. No one would hear the simple, yet dazzling story of the angel's appearance to the young girl Mary, the hush of the universe as it waited for her answer, and the sigh of relief when she is heard to say, "Here am I, the servant of the Lord: let it be with me according to your word." We would not hear the story of Jesus, the carpenter's son, who has enthralled millions of people down the centuries with his kindness, his strength, his honesty, his single-minded devotion to God's kingdom and God's people. No one would know that the desire of the everlasting hills, the hope of the ages, the suffering servant has actually already appeared and has surpassed all expectations and prophecies. We would not know that death has lost its sting, that the light has shone in our darkness and the darkness cannot overcome it. We would not know the joy of the resurrection. We might have experiences of having our hearts burning within us when we meet a stranger on the road, but we would not know what to make of it and would forget it almost as soon as it had happened.

We Christians need people who will tell the story of Jesus and of their experiences of Jesus so that we can make sense of our own experiences. A dry textbook description of someone who lived and died two thousand years ago will not feed our imaginations and arouse our desires as God wants them fed and aroused. We need people who witness to the good news, who tell the story as something real and still powerful now. This is the deepest meaning of the haunting phrase in Isaiah: "How beautiful upon the mountains are the feet of the messenger who announces peace, who brings good news, who announces salvation, who says to Zion, 'Your God reigns'" (Is 52:7). Without the telling of the story with feeling there is no good news, and our world would be a bleak place indeed. And we the sadder.

These reflections lead us to the conclusion that each one of us must be a teller of the story, that each one of us is called to be a piece of good news for those we meet. We are the Robbie Coxes of our neighborhoods, towns, and cities. We all have experiences of the power of the story of God's action in our world, of Jesus as our savior and dearest friend. We need to tell our stories. A living religion is constituted by the shared faith experiences of all those who belong to that religion, not merely by dogmas and rites and buildings, as important as these are. We all have stories of God and Jesus and the Holy Spirit to tell to one another. Admittedly, the story telling can be overdone. We do not need the compulsive talkers who bore us to death with their self-important tales. But we do need to hear the great things that God has done in our midst.

Nor do our stories have to be lengthy descriptions of "religious experiences." They can be simple stories of a good deed done by a despised Samaritan. They can use homely metaphors of the smell of baking bread or dough rising because of yeast. Here's a little story I heard recently in a homily. A Jesuit priest, working in a parish in a neighborhood

117

of mixed new immigrants in Boston, was asked at Christmas time by a Buddhist woman whether she could see his church during this special season. He invited her in to the decorated church with its manger. She asked, "Is this Christmas?" He answered, "Yes." "It's beautiful." Then he took her to the downstairs where parishioners were feeding about 175 homeless people. "Is this Christmas?" "Well, uh, yes." "It is very kind." Then they sat down for a moment, and she brought out from her bundles a little bag of oranges, offered them to him and said, "This is Christmas, too." Simple gestures bring home the experience that underlies the story.

Anyone who gives a cup of water in Christ's name tells the story. Those nameless people who daily make their way to churches throughout the world to pray privately or to participate in liturgy, in much the same way Morris Elfenbein and his old friends made their way to the synagogue each weekday, are telling the story. All the priests, religious, and lay people who daily pray the liturgical hours alone or in groups, all those who daily pray the rosary, all are part of the great number of those who tell the story. Those who feed the hungry, who protest against injustice, who speak out against the immorality of modern warfare, in the name of Jesus, keep the story alive. Indeed, I venture to say that whenever our hearts reach out to embrace the sufferings of others we are not only telling the story but also co-creating it with God. Telling the story, in other words, also enacts it.

The title of this meditation reads: "Who Will Tell the Story?" The answer that our reflections lead us to is "Everyone." At least everyone is asked to contribute to the telling of the story. No one can, like Robbie Cox, tell the whole story, but we can all contribute our part to its full telling. Let's let the story live on our lips, "Like starlings startled from a tree, / Exploding in a sky of revelation, / Deliberate and free."

Chapter 15

How Is the Cycle of Evil Broken?

> Therefore, just as sin came into the world through one
> man, and death came through sin, so death spread to
> all because all have sinned . . . (Rom 5: 12).

At least since the time of Augustine Christians have been
accustomed to the idea that original sin and the tendency to
actual sin have been passed down to each succeeding generation beginning with the sin of Adam and Eve. But not many
of us have thought much about how sin is passed on. Reflection on the human condition by social scientists may help us
to a deeper understanding not only of the history of sin, but
also of the history of grace inaugurated by Jesus.

Psychoanalysts have described a phenomenon called
"repetition compulsion," defined by Ernest Jones as "the
blind impulse to repeat earlier experiences and situations
quite irrespective of any advantage that doing so might bring
from a pleasure-pain point of view"(*Papers on Psycho-
Analysis*, 4th ed., Baltimore, Wood, 1938). For example, almost as soon as a man gets divorced from one demeaning
and emasculating woman he finds another who will treat
him the same way. In analysis it is discovered that such a
repetition compulsion finds its origin in childhood experiences with parents. Indeed, transference reactions in
psychoanalytic therapy are the outbreak within the

119

therapeutic setting of those neurotic ways of relating that have continually led to frustrating and failed relationships in life and brought the client to seek therapy in the first place. Such neurotic ways of relating have been learned in the family in early life. Moreover, the study of parents of abused children regularly shows that the parents themselves were abused children. Over and over again social scientists and therapists find that the "sins" of the fathers and mothers are indeed visited on their children. The evil or hurt that is done to one generation is passed on to the next.

In *Let This Mind Be in You* Sebastian Moore acutely notes that human beings exist because God desired them into being. Hence, we have to be desirable, lovely, good, the apple of God's eye to exist at all. Yet most, if not all, human beings do not act as though they believed in their own goodness and worth. How do we get this way? Moore lays the blame at the feet of the conditional love we all receive in our families. "You're not a good boy if you don't eat all your spinach." "Where did we get such a bad girl? You can't be one of our family." "If you don't stop that, I won't love you any more." A poor self-image leads to much unhappiness in life and to making many others unhappy as well. And parents with poor self-images will have some deleterious effect on their children.

Something similar occurs in social relations between groups. Children, for example, are not born with built-in racial, ethnic, or religious prejudice. They imbibe it with their mothers' milk, as it were, from a home and neighborhood environment poisoned by racial, ethnic, or religious slurs. "Don't play with him! He's dirty." "You can't trust a Protestant." "Let's remember Grandfather Joe who was murdered by the cowardly Catholics." "Hatfields hate us McCoys because we're better than they are." Again we see that sinful attitudes and habits of thought and action are handed down from one generation to the next.

The same pattern can be discerned in the larger picture of social structures. The disparity in wealth and quality of life between the nations of the northern hemisphere and those of the southern is based on a world social system that favors the people of the northern nations over those of the south. Indeed, the system allows the northern nations to exploit those of the south, often without either side being aware of the exploitation. With each passing generation, it seems, the poor of the southern hemisphere get poorer while their northern neighbors get richer. Moreover, most people in both hemispheres believe that the way things are is the way that they are supposed to be. Nothing will really change.

In each of these examples we can discern a sinful pattern that has a history. The sins of one generation are passed on to the next, and there seems to be a cumulative effect that is overwhelming. Sin seems to roar down the centuries like a snowball that grows larger and larger as it rolls down a mountain. We can despair of ever stopping its deadly power. The darkness does seem to be overcoming the light. Matthew Arnold summed up the feeling at the end of "Dover Beach":

> Ah, love, let us be true
> To one another! for the world, which seems
> To lie before us like a land of dreams,
> So various, so beautiful, so new,
> Hath really neither joy, nor love, nor light,
> Nor certitude, nor peace, nor help for pain;
> And we are here as on a darkling plain
> Swept with confused alarms of struggle and flight,
> Where ignorant armies clash by night.

In Romans Paul sounds a similar note.

> So I find it to be a law that when I want to do what is good, evil lies close at hand. For I delight in the law of God in my inmost self, but I see in my members another law at war with the law of my mind, making me captive to the law of sin that dwells in my mem-

121

bers. Wretched man that I am! Who will rescue me from this body of death? (Rom 7:21-24).

Paul, however, immediately answers his own question: "Thanks be to God through Jesus Christ our Lord!" For Christians believe that "The light shines in the darkness, and the darkness did not overcome it" (Jn 1:5). The letter to the Romans which we cited at the beginning of this meditation goes on to say: "But the free gift is not like the trespass. For if the many died through the one man's trespass, much more surely have the grace of God and the free gift in the grace of the one man, Jesus Christ, abounded for the many" (Rom 5:15). How does Jesus overcome the sinful pattern that seems so overpowering? In two separate sessions of spiritual direction a woman told me of an insight and an experience that may shed light on this question. She has given me permission to recount her experience.

The insight came as she was contemplating Jesus on the cross. She was behind the cross, as though looking down with Jesus on the scene in front of him. She realized that Jesus was absorbing all the hate and malice directed at him without passing it on. In other words, with Jesus the sinful pattern we have noted came to a dead halt because he did not allow it to make him a carrier. The woman also realized that anyone who really wanted to follow Jesus had to want to be like him as he accepted his passion and death. The pattern of sin is stopped when and insofar as people, by the grace of God, imitate Jesus in not becoming carriers of the contagion, when, in other words, people do not allow the sins visited on them to control their attitudes and behavior toward others.

We need to make clear that Jesus does not absorb the punishment the way a masochist or a "sad sack" would. Jesus does not get covert pleasure from his suffering, nor does he turn the hatred aimed at him into self-hatred. He is not a "victim" who feels that he deserves what he gets. So, too, the

Christian who follows Christ must not confuse masochism or the "victim" syndrome with suffering as Christ suffers.

But to suffer as Christ suffers is not an easy path, just as it was not an easy path for Jesus. A few weeks later the woman was praying in a chapel and looked at a crucifix. In her imagination she felt the horror of the crucifixion, the horrible wrenching of Jesus' body and spirit as he hung there and received the hate and malice directed at him. At one point she sensed that his face became contorted, almost demonia-cal. She was frightened and asked God to be with her. She felt a peace come over her, but she was still haunted by the image of Jesus dying so horribly. As she was telling the story, I thought of Paul's saying: "God made him who had no sin to be sin for us . . ." (2 Cor 5:21). Could it be that it was a great struggle even for the Son of God to receive all this horror and hate without passing it on? Might not the woman's image of Jesus on the cross have reflected that struggle? After all, Jesus is also human, and it is no sin to have to struggle to remain loving and forgiving toward those who torment him. But he does bring it off, thus revealing the essence of who God is for us, namely a self-sacrificing love that will not change no matter what we do to him.

If Jesus had to struggle to contain the effects of evil so that they would not spill over onto his tormentors, we who follow Jesus will know that same struggle. To forgive as Jesus for-gives, to love as Jesus loves is no cheap grace. We will want our pound of flesh for wrongs done to us. Worse yet, as we have noted, we will, all unwittingly, tend to inflict on others what has been done to us. We need to allow into conscious-ness the hurts and wrongs of our past life and to ask God to help us to forgive from the bottom of our hearts those who have inflicted them. Such healing of memories is a painful process, but one that is, I believe, necessary if we are to come to the wisdom Jesus expressed on the road to Emmaus. "Was it not necessary that the Messiah should suffer these things and then enter into his glory?" (Lk 24:26). Jesus would not be who he now is if his life had been different, if the passion had not happened to him. Not that God wanted it this way, not that Jesus wanted it this way—to say that God wanted the passion would be to say that God wanted men to kill his son, wanted them to sin. But once done, it was necessary in order that Jesus be who he now is.

Another way to understand this biblical "necessity" is indicated by Erik Erikson who calls his final developmental stage the crisis between ego integrity and despair. Ego integrity or wisdom "is the acceptance of one's one and only life cycle as something that had to be and that, by necessity, permitted of no substitutions: it thus means a new, a different love of one's parents" (*Childhood and Society*). Such a new, different love of one's parents may require a very deep forgiveness of them and of the hurts inflicted by life. Such forgiveness is not an achievement of our wills, but a grace for which we beg in prayer.

We may be tempted to conclude that such wisdom is reserved for old age. It may be true that it is more likely later in life, but the following story illustrates that the grace may be available much earlier in life. Robert and Suzanne Massie describe life with their son, Robert, who was born a hemophiliac. At nineteen Robert, Jr., was asked whether he wished that he had not had the illness. This was his reply:

How can I—or anyone—wish that the most important thing that ever happened to me had not happened? It is like saying that I wish I had been born on another planet, so different would I probably be. Put it this way: I would not have it any other way. . . . Am I rationalizing? . . . To say that would be to say that I have come through the pain and troubles of my first eighteen years with nothing to show for it. To believe that would be to believe that I learned nothing of human nature and kindness through all the years of hospitals, that my parents were unable to impart more than an average sense of faith through all my setbacks. If this were true, if having vanquished braces, bleeding, pain, self-consciousness, boredom, and depression, I have not added in any way to my appreciation of this life that has been given me, then that indeed would be a misfortune to be pitied (Robert Massie and Suzanne Massie, *Journey*. New York: Knopf, 1975).

The "sins" of the fathers and mothers are, indeed, passed to their children in many different ways. But the history of sin is not the only history we have. Even before the birth of Christ there was a history of grace, of the refusal to become a carrier of evil, of the forgiveness of enemies, of the deep acceptance of the hurts of life without passing them on. The mother of Jesus herself, the sinless one, is a product of that history of grace. But with the death and resurrection of Jesus that history has taken a new turn or dug more deeply into the marrow of human hearts and culture. In spite of the strength of the history of sin, a strength that seems to grow more implacable with the centuries, "There lives," as Gerard Manley Hopkins says, "the dearest freshness deep down things," the Spirit of Jesus who makes it possible for wounded mortals like ourselves to pass on care and love and thoughtfulness rather than fear, prejudice, hatred, and abuse. "Because the Holy Ghost over the bent / World broods with warm breast and with ah! bright wings."

Part 4

Discernment and Action

Chapter 16

Discernment and Obedience: Finding God's Will and Staying Roman Catholic

Discernment has become a buzz word among people who know Ignatian spirituality. "I discerned that God wants me to become provincial." (Obviously, the man is crazy.) "I discerned that I should teach poor children in Guatemala." (But she has proven totally incapable of learning any foreign language.) The word discernment has been used to persuade superiors into letting people do what they want to do, as in: "I discerned that I should study for a doctorate in Sanskrit; I feel great peace when I contemplate such study and sense that God is calling me to that work." The superior may not see any need for a Sanskrit scholar in the province, but if he or she denies the request, the person may say that the superior is thwarting the will of God. I knew a Jesuit priest who discerned himself out of the Roman Catholic Church, supposedly using Ignatian principles. Then, of course, there is the Jesuit provincial—perhaps mythical—who said: "You discern, I decide."

Discernment refers to a way of discovering God's will for me in my own personal experience. And yet, those who know Ignatian spirituality may wonder whether discernment has any place in it at all. After all, Ignatius and the Jesuit order he founded have been known in the church for their stress on obedience. Ignatius wrote a rather famous letter on obedience in which he said, among other things, that the subject should follow the least sign of the superior's will, that a Jesuit should consider himself like a blind man's staff to be used in any way that superiors saw fit. In his *Spiritual Exercises* he has a series of rules for thinking with the church. In one of these he says: "If we wish to proceed securely in all things, we must hold fast to the following principle: What seems to me white, I will believe black if the hierarchical Church so defines." With such a strong emphasis on obedience there seems no place for individual discernment in Ignatian spirituality. So if you want to stay Roman Catholic, why not just obey and forget all this business of discernment?

However, in the same *Spiritual Exercises* Ignatius has an even longer set of rules for the discernment of spirits. The purpose of these rules is to help a retreatant to discern, within the different interior affects and thoughts, what God is drawing him or her to do in life. So within the very book that is seen as the source of his spirituality we find a tension between discernment and obedience. I want to show that this tension is what makes Ignatian spirituality authentically Catholic and still needed in the church today.

After his recuperation from a terrible battle wound and his conversion to following Christ, Ignatius spent ten months in the little town of Manresa being taught by God, as he himself later said. This ten-month period formed the basis of what he later distilled in the book of the *Spiritual Exercises*. During this time he became convinced (he discerned) that God wanted him to live out his life "following Christ poor." Moreover, he was absolutely sure that God wanted him to live out his life in the Holy Land. So with this set purpose he made his way to Jerusalem, as he tells us in his *Autobiography*. There he met with the provincial of the Franciscans and told him of his firm intention to remain in Jerusalem. The provincial told him flatly that he could not remain and had to leave the next day, giving him many reasons for the decision. Ignatius says:

> [I] replied that [my] decision to remain was fixed and that nothing could prevent [me] from carrying it out. With great honesty [I] gave the provincial to understand that though the provincial did not agree with [me], and since this was not a matter that obliged under sin, [I] would not renounce [my] plans out of fear.

The provincial then told Ignatius that he had the power from the Holy See to expel or keep anyone he chose, and to excommunicate anyone who refused to obey. So here Ignatius came smack up against the tension between discernment and obedience. On the one hand, he had become convinced through his own discernment of spirits that God wanted him to follow the poor Christ in the Holy Land. On the other hand, someone who had authority in the church was telling him that he could not remain in the Holy Land, and telling him in the strongest way, namely by threatening excommunication. How did Ignatius come to a decision? He decided, as he says, that "it was not God's will for him to remain in the Holy Places."

Apparently, for Ignatius, if it came to a point where obedience to the voice of discernment would lead to his being separated from the church, then he would conclude that some part of his discernment was mistaken. In fact, this conflict with the Franciscan provincial posed a brand new question for Ignatius, namely, how to live out his clear call to follow the poor Christ as an apostle. Ultimately, he was led, by trial and error, to found, with nine young companions, the Society of Jesus. If he had refused to obey the provincial, there would, in all likelihood, be no St. Ignatius of Loyola, no

Society of Jesus, and none of the institutions and history associated with the Society of Jesus since 1540.

What I want to underline is that there was, and is, a real tension between personal discernment and obedience. Ignatius did not give in to the provincial at the first indication of his will. He pushed his determination to the point where it came down to obeying or being excommunicated. Moreover, he did not completely give up the idea of returning to the Holy Land and remaining there. In fact, thirteen years later he and his first companions tried for a whole year to get to the Holy Land and only when it became clear that no ships would be going there did they go to Rome and offer themselves to the Pope. No matter what Ignatius said about obedience, his practice shows that when he was convinced of what God wanted him to do or of what God wanted for the Society he founded, he would do all in his power to convince the one who had authority of this, but finally obey when he had done all that he could. And he obeyed peacefully and without hidden resentment, convinced that God would see things through.

Moreover, while he treated authority with respect, his respect never veered toward being a mere "yes man." One example will suffice for many. When Ignatius was studying in Alcala and "helping souls" with his Exercises, he was investigated for heresy by a prelate named Figueroa who found nothing heretical in what he was doing. However, Figueroa put some restrictions on Ignatius and his companions. Ignatius said that they would obey as long as they were in his jurisdiction. "But," he added, "I do not know how beneficial such investigations are. The other day a priest refused to give the Sacrament to one of us because he receives Communion every week, and they have made difficulties for me. We would like to know whether they have found any heresy in us." Figueroa answered: "No; if they had, they would have burned you." "They would have likewise burned you," Ignatius retorted, "if they found heresy in you."

In other words, Ignatius was a bone-deep member of the church who believed that his salvation came in and through this church. To leave it was unthinkable. At the same time, he was an adult, not a child, in the church, an adult who believed that God could and did communicate to him a direction and a way of life that would also be helpful to others. He lived out the tension that can come from the polarities of obedience and discernment. Ignatius could only remain authentically Christian and Catholic by holding in tension these polarities. I am convinced that the spirituality he discovered has perennial value for the church, and especially at this historic time in the church when, just as in Ignatius' time, a world order is crumbling and all of us must seek with adult honesty, humility, and courage God's new way for the forward movement of this world. We need to become adult discerners of the ways of God and communicate honestly and openly what we discern, and at the same time stay anchored in the Roman Catholic church where alone for us salvation is found.

Chapter 17

Should Religion Concern Itself With Political and Social Issues?

When John XXIII's social encyclical *Mater et Magistra* appeared in 1961, one of the more famous ripostes was William Buckley's "Mater, si; Magistra, no." Whenever religious leaders make statements about political matters, they are reminded by some critics that their place is in the sacristy, not the marketplace. The bishops of the United States were roundly criticized in some circles for even taking up the topics of nuclear warfare and the economy in recent years. And John Paul II's *Sollicitudo Rei Socialis (On Social Concern)* issued near the end of 1987 raised a furor even before some of the critics had read it. On a few occasions I have heard people angrily argue that they go to church on Sunday to find peace and consolation, not sermons on social justice. Again the clear implication is that the church is no place for the discussion of political matters.

To be truthful about it, Catholic teaching which distinguishes the natural order from the supernatural order and the secular from the sacred makes these criticisms plausible. If there is a real distinction between the natural and the supernatural orders, then religion has to do primarily with the supernatural and only secondarily with the natural order. The natural order comes into the purview of religion only insofar as what is done in the natural order affects one's standing in the supernatural order. Just as the military say, "Leave war to the generals," so too businessmen would say, "Leave business to businessmen," and politicians, "Leave politics to the politicians." Indeed, if there is a real distinction between the natural and supernatural orders, the only legitimate concerns of religion as such in the natural order are the individual morality of those who act in the natural order and the freedom of the church to carry out its functions.

In a number of lectures and written works the late Scottish philosopher John Macmurray argued strongly that religion, and specifically Christianity, was infected with a dualism that could destroy its effectiveness in meeting the central challenge of our time, the development of a universal community of men and women. In the Essex Hall Lecture of 1944, *Idealism Against Religion*, for example, he begins by noting the decline of religious influence and opines that "all of us, within and without the churches, are losing or have lost the capacity to think and feel religiously, and to behave religiously." The cause of the calamity, he believes, is idealism. "For it is my belief that religion and idealism are enemies, and at war with one another: that idealism is a disease of the spirit which infects its marrow, and as it spreads it blinds us to the reality of the religious life, and shuts us up in the world of our sick fantasies" (pp. 5-6). Since these lectures are so seminal and yet so difficult to find, I want to develop his argument in order to show not only that religious leaders may legitimately speak in the "marketplace," but that they must if religion is to be real.

By idealism Macmurray does not mean the readiness to believe in, hope in and act for the good. For instance, we might call someone an idealist and mean thereby that the person tries to bring about the change of unjust social structures. The idealism Macmurray castigates consists "in an emotional attachment to ideas rather than to things" (p. 8). An idealist in this sense has little drive to change things. As

136

a result of the emotional attachment to ideas, activities which concern ideas are preferred to activities concerned with material objects and are valued for their own sake rather than for their relation to material objects. (By things and material objects Macmurray means actual beings in the world.) Dualism follows immediately. The world is no longer one world, but two, the material world and the spiritual world, and since we have to live in both worlds, we have two lives, a life of the mind and a life of the body, a life in this world and a life in another world. I believe that the real distinction between the natural and the supernatural orders, that is, the idea that these are two separate entities, derives from this dualism.

> When idealism makes conquest of religion, religion becomes concerned with the other life, the spiritual life; and with the other world which is so different from this. Thus when we fall a prey to idealism we distinguish the material from the spiritual, and set them in opposition; and the root of this is that we value ideas above things; so that instead of recognizing that ideas are about things, we behave as if things were about ideas; and our religion begins to treat this world as if it were for the sake of the other, and referred to it (p. 11).

Religious idealism uses the imagination to create an ideal world in which human beings would be fully satisfied. As a result the ideal world is a world of things as they ought to be, not as they are; hence a better world, one where poverty, suffering, and death do not exist. Since, however, this ideal world has no relation to the real world in which we must, perforce, exist, it gives us no clues on how to act in this world to make it conform more and more to the ideal world. In fact, the temptation of the religious idealist is to withdraw from the real world, to let it go to the devil, as it were. As Macmurray says, "a religion which has succumbed to idealism is other-worldly. . . . Because it is not about this world, it exists

137

for our comfort and satisfaction. It is our refuge from the sorrows and the evils of this life, and we retire from the world to enter the realm of ideas and images which it has built for our consolation" (p. 17).

The argument against idealism in religion comes to a head in these pithy comments explaining the decline of religious influence in our day.

> Religious idealism can appeal to two classes of people; those for whom there is no immediate urgency to change the conditions of ordinary life, because they are reasonably satisfied with it as it is; and those to whom the conditions of life are very unsatisfying, but who see no possibility of doing anything to change them. It can make no appeal to those for whom change is urgent, and who believe that it can be brought about through human effort. In our time the urgency of change increases for growing masses of people, and the belief in the possibility of effecting it spreads more and more widely (p. 18).

Marx's critique of religion as the opium of the people applies to religious idealism as Macmurray describes it.

This idealism permeates our thinking about religion. It lies, I believe, behind the criticisms leveled at popes, bishops, priests, and other Christians who speak religiously and pointedly to the institutions and structures of our world. Some would say that what Macmurray describes as religious idealism is in fact Christian doctrine. After all, Jesus did say: "My kingdom is not of this world." Is it possible for a Roman Catholic to think any other way about the nature of Christianity?

First, it is well to recall that scripture scholars generally agree that for Jesus the kingdom of God is not an other-worldly hope. With the words just cited, Jesus does not mean that the kingdom is or will be located someplace else, but that its origins and values are from God, are immanent only as transcendent.

Second, the distinction between the natural and the super-natural orders does not have to lead to thinking of them as two distinct worlds. The purpose of the distinction, I believe, is to underscore the gratuity of the supernatural order. That is, God could have created a universe in which the offer of divine intimacy (sanctifying grace, the beatific vision, community with God himself) was not offered. Such a world would have been a "natural" world, not a "supernatural" world. But in point of fact God created a universe in which the offer of divine intimacy is ever-present. Hence, the real world in which we live and work and play is through and through supernatural. Indeed, Karl Rahner coined the term "supernatural existential" precisely to make the point that whether or not an individual accepts God's offer of intimacy or even knows that there is a God who makes such an offer, that person still is the object of God's loving invitation at every moment of existence.

Third, by revelation we do know what God wants of this universe. As noted before, God wants a universe in which all people live in community with the Trinity and hence as brothers and sisters of one another. This intention, it seems, governs his one action which is the universe. And the theater for this community is this universe, not some other world. Macmurray puts it this way: "If it were cured of idealism, religion would be about this world, and not about any other world. Its beliefs would provide an interpretation of the common life of humanity, and would find their evidence in history and common experience; not in special experiences and strange visions" (p. 18). In this world and no other God wants us all to live as brothers and sisters of Jesus and of one another, and our task is to bend every effort to find effective ways to live in harmony with God's intention. We work out our salvation precisely in the marketplace.

The very fact that we must work out effective ways to live in harmony with God's intention in this real world means that we must do more than pray. We must also get to know

139

this real world in all its concrete detail. It would be another form of religious idealism to try to pronounce on economic, social, and political issues without getting acquainted with them in all their complexity. The American bishops gave us an admirable example of religious realism in the way they went about writing their pastoral letters on nuclear arms and the economy.

Let me conclude with another trenchant paragraph from *Idealism Against Religion.*

> Instead of thinking about religious things we should think about ordinary things in a religious way. Instead of living a spiritual life which is separate from and in opposition to our material life we should live our ordinary life spiritually. Instead of believing in the idea of God, we should seek and find God in this world—a God who does not depend on us and our believings or disbelievings, but on whom we depend. Our religion would cease to be for our comfort or consolation, a compensation for the futilities and failure of our material life, and become power and knowledge for the salvation of the world through us, and even at our expense (p. 18-19).

In other words, if we were to think about ordinary things in a religious way, we would become what Ignatius of Loyola called contemplatives in action, people who find God in all things. And we would rejoice that our religious leaders look for the presence or absence of God precisely in the marketplace. We might, of course, disagree with their discernment of what constitutes God's presence in the structures and institutions of our world, but even our disagreement would underscore that they not only have a right to speak to political and social issues but must do so if they are to be true to their Lord whose kingdom is not of this world, but yet is in this real world.

As I understand it, the Church teaches that our resurrected bodies will be intact as to personality, that is,
intact with all the contradictions beautiful to you,
except the contradiction of sin; sin is the contradiction, the interference, of a greater good by a lesser
good. I look for all variety in that unity but not for a
choice: for when all you see will be God, all you will
want will be God.

> From a letter of Flannery O'Connor
> to "A" 16 Dec 1955
> *The Habit of Being*, Sally Fitzgerald, ed.

Annotated Bibliography

Barry, William A. *God and You: Prayer as a Personal Relationship*. Mahwah, NJ: Paulist Press, 1987.

_____. *"Seek My Face:" Prayer as Personal Relationship in Scripture*. Mahwah, NJ: Paulist Press, 1989.

_____. *Paying Attention to God: Discernment in Prayer*. Notre Dame, IN: Ave Maria Press, 1990.

_____. *"Now Choose Life": Conversion as the Way to Life*. Mahwah, NJ: Paulist Press, 1990.

_____. *Finding God in All Things: A Companion to the Spiritual Exercises of St. Ignatius*. Notre Dame, IN: Ave Maria Press, 1991.

Buechner, Frederick. *The Sacred Journey*. San Francisco: Harper & Row, 1982. An autobiographical memoir whose aim is to show how God has spoken in the ordinary events of his life.

De Waal, Esther. *Every Earthly Blessing: Celebrating a Spirituality of Creation*. Ann Arbor, MI: Servant Publications, 1992. Drawing on the Celtic tradition the author presents prayers and blessings that indicate a deep faith in ordinary Celtic Catholics that God can be found in all things.

Hall, Thelma. *Too Deep for Words: Rediscovering Lectio Divina*. Mahwah, NJ: Paulist Press, 1988. A very practical little book to help people pray with scripture. Includes 500 scripture texts for prayer.

Hillesum, Etty. *An Interrupted Life: The Diaries of Etty Hillesum 1941-43*. New York: Washington Square Press, 1985. One of the finest testaments to the triumph of love over fear and hatred I have read.

Moore, Sebastian. *Let This Mind Be in You: The Quest for Identity Through Oedipus to Christ.* San Francisco: Harper & Row (Seabury), 1985. A dense but brilliant work by one of the most original spiritual theologians writing today.

_____. *Jesus the Liberator of Desire.* New York: Crossroad, 1989. The brilliant sequel to *Let This Mind Be in You* in which Moore once again explores the meaning of the death and resurrection of Jesus for our lives.

O'Connor, Flannery. *The Habit of Being: Letters of Flannery O'Connor.* Sally Fitzgerald, ed. New York: Farrar, Straus, Giroux, 1979. These letters are insightful, poignant, spiritually and esthetically wise, witty, down-to-earth, and, at times, enough to make you laugh out loud. My end quote indicates the depth of her spirituality.

Williams, H. A. *True Resurrection.* New York: Holt, Rinehart, Winston, 1972. The author maintains that unless the resurrection is experienced in our real lives now, it is a dogma that has no relevance for us. He shows by examples from ordinary experience that we do experience resurrection now.